Author's Note:-

I write this book because I want to write a book from a long time may be before six months. Now I quit my job to live a life I want to. I just want to share my experience of life—nothing more, nothing less. I'm simply expressing myself. I believe everyone has something to say, stories worth telling. These are mine but not the stories because I don't trust in stories just focus on SAAR. So reviled something and decorate on Sutras.

Read them like you sip a drink—enjoy it, feel it, and then forget it.

Buddha said a lot. His words held deep meaning, but he died a long time ago. I understand his message, but I don't believe there's a need to follow him anymore. What remains are distorted versions of the original teachings. I've chosen to decline the paths laid out by others. I follow only myself now—with no doubt, no hesitation.

This is your story too—live it fully. Live dangerously.

Don't cling to what's written here. Don't judge it. Don't even hold on to it. Just let it be.

I'm not claiming this is right or wrong. I've simply said what I wanted to say—from my soul.

If it reaches to your soul, so my writing is successful. I am neither a theist nor atheist, I am just a watcher and I write what I watch. Read it be like watcher, take an absolute view.

Specials Thanks: -

My father: Mr. Omkar Prashad Tiwari

My Mother: Mrs. Lata Tiwari

My poetic sense.

When the light falls down, Darkness spreads everywhere

When the darkness known itself, So why we need the light.

Although darkness means unknown, It's better to be in absurd light.

When the darkness is deep around, Again we urge to find the light.

Distorted light have different colours while the darkness know as black.

When the all colours of light rivals, again become the dark.

Light means to be known, but what we comprehend May different.

Light have the different prospective. But darkness have only one.

Pain ends with light but happiness ends on darkness. Lies ends with light while truth ends on darkness.

Darkness is rigid hence light is versatile. Both are our ally when we have the sight.

<u>The Sutra's of Yogi</u>

A journey from being a human to becoming a Universal Being.

1.The Believe System Trap.   **Pg 5.**

2. Be Alone.   **Pg 42**

3.Labelling is useless.   **Pg 79**

4. Love is the only way.   **Pg 111**

5. Dhyan to Dharmikta .   **Pg 142**

<u>**Sutra - 1**</u>

Belief: A Powerful Tool That Can Work For or Against You

Belief is one of the most powerful tools a human being can possess. It can do anything **for** you—or **against** you. It has the power to elevate or to destroy, depending on how it's used.

To **believe** means you've accepted something as truth. And the moment you accept something as truth without question, you stop inquiring. Once questioning stops, intelligence starts to fade. A mind that no longer questions becomes vulnerable—open to manipulation and exploitation.

Take a simple example: fire.
If you put your hand in fire, it burns. This is direct experience. Through this experience, you become a believer in the fact that fire causes pain. But you also learn that fire has another side—it gives off heat, which can be useful for warmth or cooking food. This is a **healthy belief**, rooted in reality and personal understanding. You've seen both the danger and the usefulness of fire.

Now imagine someone comes along—a so-called spiritual guru—and tells you,

"This fire is holy. God has said it will burn away your impurities. Even if it gives you blisters, you will become pure."

At first, it sounds mystical, maybe even inspiring. But if you truly believe this without questioning it, you might willingly burn your hand in that fire, thinking it will make you holy. Even if your hand is blistered, even if you can't eat with it for weeks, you will accept the suffering—not because it's necessary, but because you **believe** it's divine.

This is **blind belief**.

Blind belief is when you stop trusting your own eyes, your own intelligence, your own experience—and put your faith entirely in someone else's words or authority. And when belief turns blind, it no longer frees you. It binds you.

The Inherited Path: Are We Living Our Truth or Someone Else's?

In today's world, before a child even takes their first breath, their life has already been written. A name, a religion, a belief system, a set of rules — all assigned at birth. The child is not born free, but born into a **pre-decided identity**. And this identity is rarely questioned.

By the time a child learns to speak, society has already whispered into their ears who they are supposed to be. If born into a Christian family, they are told they are a follower of Christ and must know the teachings of the Bible, attend church, and follow Christian customs. If born into a Muslim household, the Quran becomes their holy book, and they are expected to follow the Five Pillars of Islam, visit the mosque, and honour the prophet Muhammad. A child born into a Hindu family is introduced to Krishna, the Bhagavad Gita, temples, and countless rituals — all as part of their "natural" identity.

But the question arises: **Is this truly our belief, or a belief we inherited without choice?**

The Problem of Inherited Belief

The danger lies not in religion itself, but in the **automatic acceptance** of belief without inquiry. These belief systems may carry profound wisdom, but when adopted blindly, they become chains rather than tools for growth.

The moment belief becomes fixed and unquestioned, **intelligence starts to fade**. We stop observing the world with our own eyes and start seeing it through the lens of someone else's truth.

And in this, our unique essence gets buried beneath layers of inherited programming.

Let's take the example of **Malala Yousafzai**, the young Pakistani girl who defied the norms of her society. Born in a conservative region where girls were discouraged from education, her path was supposed to be predetermined — quiet, obedient, uneducated. But she **questioned**. She believed that education was her right. That act of defiance nearly cost her life, but it also ignited a global movement. Malala did not follow the path laid out for her; she **carved her own**.

Similarly, **Galileo Galilei** dared to challenge the teachings of the Church when he supported the heliocentric model — that the Earth revolves around the Sun. The dominant belief at the time, backed by religious authority, claimed the opposite. Galileo's insistence on truth, based on observation and reason, earned him house arrest. Yet today, we see him as a hero of science — someone who chose truth over tradition.

Great philosophers have always encouraged us to ask deeper questions. Socrates, considered the father of Western philosophy, famously said:

"The unexamined life is not worth living."

Buddha walked away from his royal palace in search of truth, leaving behind all the beliefs he had inherited. His journey wasn't about adopting a new system — it was about discovering what is **real** through direct experience.

The same is true of mystics like **Kabir**, who questioned both Hindu and Muslim rituals, urging people to look beyond labels and institutions to find the divine within.

In a world that prides itself on freedom, we must ask:
Are we really free if we are born into belief without choice?
We are taught what to think, but rarely how to think. We memorize holy books, but rarely explore their deeper meaning for ourselves. We are given answers before we even know how to ask the questions.

This creates a society of followers, not seekers.

This book is not a rejection of religion, culture, or tradition. These can be beautiful, meaningful parts of life. But they should be chosen, not forced. They should evolve with understanding, not be followed out of fear or habit.

Every individual deserves the chance to explore, question, and rediscover truth in their own way. That's where real growth begins — not by following the map, but by walking the path with awareness.

 These systems are pre-decided nobody will ask you like:-

 Hey kid we have some kind of Religion would you like to follow anyone of these.

so, he may reply; why we need to follow one of these?

Because everyone on this planet have at least one of them.

He replays: but why?

Because there is almighty GOD who creates the world of us, create everything so we must worship him, if you worshipping him.

everything will go right or he may save you from further miss-happening.

He: Which GOD is more powerful?

Here we lying: Of course, our GOD.

He: Innocent KID believes on it, ok then I will follow the same but before I follow, can you please explain me why people follow the other religion if your god is great why would they not follow as ours?

Again lies: Because their GOD create them and our GOD create us.

He: How many GODS out there or why our GOD is so supreme? If GODs create us so who will create the GOD?

Here we divert him: You do not need to worry about it, things are like this just do the same as we did.

From there any question which we are unable to answer or do not know, we put on the GOD.

The Script of Society:-

This is not your journey,
It is a script you inherited.
A life carved out of someone else's story.
Not a path you walked —
But one laid before you,
Stone by stone,
By voices you never chose to follow.

And the world applauds when you walk it blindly.
They call it devotion.
They call it loyalty.
But never ask —
Is it freedom?

The Illusion of Divinity and the Shelter of Religion

Our lies may delay the truth for a while, but eventually, he will arrive at the inevitable conclusion: there is no God outside. The idea of God is not something tangible or absolute—it is the creation of human imagination. It is our response to the unknown, the incomprehensible, and the uncontrollable aspects of existence. Whenever we are faced with something we cannot explain or influence, we place it in the hands of a higher power—we call it "God."

Religion is an umbrella and God is need to support the umbrella and all the people who follow the same religion is standing under the Umbrella. So, they said do not look outside and do not even think to go outside there is a heavy rain outside, we all are surrounding with the heavy thunder storm. People also believe in that or by fear, they follow every instruction given by the religion. In reality, what we understand as religion is simply a gathering of people who share the same customs, culture, and collective fears. Religion is not necessarily about divine truth—it is a system, a tradition, a civilization's way of organizing life, giving meaning to suffering, and creating a sense of belonging. It acts as an umbrella—broad, encompassing, and sheltering. At the center of this umbrella stands the idea of God, holding it up. The people, bound by common beliefs, gather underneath, clinging to the safety it offers.

But the shelter comes with rules. They are told: *Do not look outside. Do not even think of stepping beyond this cover. There is a heavy rain outside—a violent thunderstorm that will consume you.* And so, many accept this warning without question. Whether through belief or fear, they obey the instructions given by religion. It is easier to follow than to question. Easier to stay dry than to risk the unknown storm.

But the truth is, the storm is not always real. Sometimes it is exaggerated. Sometimes it is fabricated to keep people inside, to maintain order, control, and tradition. And yet, some will still dare to look beyond. They will notice the cracks in the shelter. They will feel the drops of rain and begin to wonder if the world outside is truly as terrifying as they were taught.

Eventually, they may come to realize that God is not an external being, but a reflection of human fear and hope. That religion, while rich in culture and tradition, is a man-made structure. A beautiful one, perhaps. A meaningful one. But not necessarily divine.

And in that realization, there is both liberation and responsibility. Without an external God to dictate right and wrong, we must define our own morality. Without the umbrella, we must face the storm on our own. But perhaps, in doing so, we might discover that the rain is not the enemy—but the beginning of something more honest, more human, and more free.

The Chains of Blind Belief and the Need for Understanding

Civilization, since its early days, has relied on systems—systems of belief, power, and tradition— to guide people along a predefined path. Religion, one of the most influential of these systems, has played a significant role in shaping human behavior and social order for thousands of years. And while it is not inherently wrong to follow religious or cultural traditions, it becomes dangerous when we follow them blindly.

Blind belief is a silent killer of both freedom and thought. It leads people away from their own reasoning, from their ability to question and choose, and places them in a position where they can be easily manipulated. Exploitation thrives in such an environment. When people are taught *not* to think but only to obey, they lose not only their individual dignity but risk the future of their children as well. We must ask ourselves: if we don't understand *why* we believe in something, then are we truly living? Or are we merely surviving within the boundaries set by others?

Take for instance the rigid structures within Hinduism. From the moment of birth, one is labeled—Brahmin, Kshatriya, Vaishya, or Shudra—and society expects them to live within the limits of that label for their entire life. No exceptions. No questions. This is not just a religious identity; it becomes a life sentence. And this division doesn't stop at religion. We further separate ourselves by nations, by class, by wealth. The rich are seen as powerful, the middle class as striving, the poor as invisible. Even among the middle class, there are layers—upper, lower, daily wage earners. The hierarchy is endless.

But in my view, the poorest of all are not those who lack money—but those who blindly follow others without ever using their own mind. Intelligence is nature's gift, and to waste it on mindless obedience is to live in slavery. How can we call someone truly human if they give up the very gift that defines our humanity—conscious thought?

And then we wonder: where is love in such a society? A society built on division, comparison, and fear—how can it create harmony? How can love thrive when people are judged by their caste, their bank account, their religion, or the place of their birth? The truth is, it cannot.

Real harmony, real love, comes only from understanding. From people seeing each other as fellow human beings, not as members of a label or system. We must awaken from this mental sleep and learn to question what we follow. Not to rebel blindly, but to understand deeply. Only then can we build a society where people are truly free—not just to believe, but to think, to feel, and to love.

The System, the Script, and the Death of the Self

From the moment we are born, we are handed an identity. Before we even speak our first word, society begins to script our life. We are placed into a system—a structure so deeply ingrained that most never even realize they are a part of it. Every major decision of our life is already made for us: go to school, get good grades, find a respectable job, get married, raise children, work until old age, and then quietly leave the world. This is the cycle we are expected to follow, without question.

If you follow this path, they will call you a *good child*, a *responsible adult*. But the moment you step out of line—if you dare to dream differently or live by your own rules—the world begins to resist you. Society will question you, but before that, your own parents might. You'll be labeled difficult, rebellious, even selfish. The system is not designed for individuality; it is designed for obedience.

As a child, you're told what success looks like. You're pressured to perform, to compete, to achieve. Once your education is complete, you're told to find a job—not necessarily one that fulfills you, but one that pays. To marry, not necessarily for love, but for tradition. To raise a family, not necessarily because you want to, but because it's expected. And in this process, you repeat the cycle.

You plan the future of your children just as yours was planned for you.

You spend your life in motion, ticking boxes, fulfilling duties—and then, one day, you're old. Death begins to approach, silently. And in those final moments, a question often arises in the soul: *Did I do everything right? Did I fulfill my responsibilities?*

But what if a deeper question starts to echo: *Did I ever live freely? Did I ever choose for myself?* You begin to realize that perhaps, all along, you were simply following. Following the voice of your father, your religion, your family, your society. And never once stopping to ask: *What do I want?*

We live like machines—efficient, predictable, responsible—but without love, passion, or fire. No time to feel deeply, to live wildly, or to breathe freely. We are taught to fear our own desires, to silence our inner voice, to distrust our instincts. And why? Because freedom is dangerous. Freedom threatens the system. It requires courage—the kind that many have been trained to suppress from birth.

And so we stay inside the box. Born into it, living in it, and dying in it.

To live this way is not to live as a creation of God or the universe—it is to live as a creation of the system. A manufactured life, produced by culture, expectations, and fear. It's a life where we trust everyone else—parents, priests, politicians—but not ourselves.

But what if we changed that? What if we paused and truly listened—not to the noise of the world, but to the quiet whisper within? The soul knows. The heart remembers. The path may be harder, lonelier, full of risk—but it will be yours. And that is the only life worth living: one where you were not just a follower, but a conscious creator of your destiny.

The Financial Trap: Freedom Sold in Installments

Take another look at the system we live in—not just socially, not just spiritually, but economically. We are told from a young age that education is the path to success. So we go to school, then to college, and we pursue degrees and scholarships, believing that each certificate is a step closer to "freedom." But what kind of freedom?

We are taught to chase financial independence, as if earning money will free us from worry, struggle, or dependence. But the moment we start earning, a new cycle begins—the cycle of *spending*. You finally get a job, and naturally, you want to fulfill your desires. You buy your first bike, your first car, your first home. Maybe you don't have enough saved yet, so you take a loan. Now comes the **EMI**—the monthly installment that whispers, *you don't own it yet, but you will... one day.*

And so you work. You work to pay off the loan. Three years, five years, maybe more. Once it's paid off, there's something else you want—because desire is endless. Another car, a better house, a vacation, new gadgets. And the EMI cycle begins again. The trap tightens.

At first, you worked to gain freedom. But now, you must keep working—whether you love your job or hate it—because there are payments to make, expectations to meet. Slowly, the job becomes not a choice, but a **necessity**. You no longer work for growth—you work for survival within the lifestyle you've built.

This is the paradox of modern life: we pursue financial freedom, and end up in a **financial cage**. We are sold the dream of freedom through ownership—but in truth, ownership often owns us.

The most dangerous part? It looks normal. Everyone's doing it. Everyone's chasing. Everyone's busy. So you don't question it—until one day, you realize your whole life was spent paying for things you thought would make you happy, but only demanded more of your time, your energy, and your soul.

We have to ask: is this really freedom? Or just another form of slavery, dressed in the clothes of comfort?

The Myth of "Later" and the Courage to Live Now

Suppose you have a personal dream. A passion project. A goal that lights up your soul—something that gives your life deep meaning. But you're caught in the system, paying EMIs, stuck in a job you may not love. And so you tell yourself, *"Once my loans are paid, I will begin."* Or, *"I'll work on my dream in my spare time."*

But let me be honest with you—this is just a **myth**. A lie we tell ourselves to feel better while postponing what matters most. You cannot ride two horses at once. You cannot walk the path of the soul while chained to a system that demands your time, your energy, and your spirit.

Every day you delay, every moment you tell yourself "not now," you're giving away a piece of yourself. The truth is: **dreams are not for the fearful**. They are not for those waiting for the "right time"—because there is no right time. There is only *now*.

Dreams belong to those who have the **courage to live dangerously**, to walk into uncertainty with open arms. These are not ordinary people. They are the **Yogis**, the **warriors** of existence. They do not live for comfort or applause. They do not ask, *"Will I succeed?"* Instead, they ask, *"Am I alive?"* And that's all that matters.

They don't care for results, for destination. Their joy is in the **journey**, in the risk, in the sweat and the setbacks. They embrace suffering—not as punishment, but as part of the dance. Their pain becomes their teacher. Their failures become their fuel. The world may call them mad, but they are the ones who **truly live**.

This path is not for everyone. It requires the death of the small self—the one addicted to comfort, security, reputation. It demands a fire inside, a hunger for truth that burns stronger than the fear of loss.

But for those who choose this path, life reveals its true face—not a routine of duties and regrets, but a wild, beautiful, unpredictable adventure.

When Life Becomes a Cage and Death Laughs at You

If you're still telling yourself, *"I'll start working on my dream once my EMIs are paid,"* you're already living in an illusion. Because life doesn't wait. Time doesn't pause. The system doesn't care about your passions, and freedom doesn't come wrapped in a paycheck.

By the time you start to clear one debt, you're pulled into the next. And just when you think you've made space to breathe, you're in your 30s. Suddenly, the system rears its head again—*"Time to get married,"* it whispers. Parents get older. Expectations rise. And everyone around you reminds you of what's "logical": marry someone nice, someone stable, someone who wants a *better life.* Translation? More money. More responsibility. More compromise.

So you prepare. You climb the career ladder. You upgrade your lifestyle. You play the role. And once you get married, you've completed half the loop. You're 50% trapped. The rest? You already know—

family, children, school fees, house loans, emergencies, sacrifices. A never-ending loop.

You might convince yourself that *one day*, you'll return to your dream. But dreams have an expiry date. By the time you're in your 60s, you're exhausted. Your body begins to falter. Your willpower fades. What once lit you up now feels like a burden. And worst of all—you've become a stranger to yourself.

You were a good son, a good father, a good husband. But somewhere along the way, you forgot to be a good *human being*. You forgot to be *you*.

The pride of a lion belongs in the jungle, not in a circus. Yet here we are—trained, obedient, performing tricks for applause, never asking who put us in the cage. And when death comes—and it *will*—you might beg for more time. You might say, *"Wait! I haven't lived yet!"* But Yamraj, the lord of death, doesn't care about your excuses. He'll say coldly, *"You had your chance. You chose this."* Then he'll pull your soul from your body—and no one can stop it. Not your parents, not your partner, not your children. No one.

You see, it's not death we should fear. It's *dying with regret*. Dying with dreams still buried inside us.

Dying without ever knowing what true freedom felt like. Without ever daring to live for the soul, not just the system.

So if this stirs fear in your heart—**good**. That fear is a sign you're still alive. If you're not scared yet, wait. You will be. Either now, while you still have time—or later, when it's too late.

Let my words be a dynamite—not to destroy your life, but to demolish the false foundation you've built it on. I don't want you to stay comfortable. I want you to *wake up*. Tear the blindfold off. Smash the illusion that "everything is fine." Stop settling for survival. Start demanding *life*.

Don't be afraid to break the cycle. Don't be afraid to dream radically, love fully, live wildly. Don't behave like you're powerless. You are not.

Because the truth is brutal: if you're not living for your soul, you're wasting your life.

Sutra One: Do Not Believe in Anything—Be a Light Unto Yourself

Do not believe in anything. Not even in your parents.

This may sound harsh, even disrespectful, but look closer: your parents are not gods. They are human beings, bound by their own fears, their own beliefs, and the limitations of the system they were raised in. They love you, yes—but love without awareness can still be blind. They will guide you only within the boundaries they know. But what if your life demands something *outside* that boundary?

I'm not saying their intentions are bad. I'm saying **intentions are not enough**. A well-meaning lie is still a lie. And blind guidance—no matter how loving—can still lead you into darkness.

Belief makes people blind. It kills questions. It replaces intelligence with obedience. Once you believe blindly, you no longer see—you only follow. And in following, you surrender your responsibility to think, to feel, to *know* for yourself.

Belief becomes psychological slavery—a quiet surrender to the comfort of certainty.

But comfort can be a cage.

Look around you. See what people are doing in the name of belief—belief in religion, belief in employment systems, belief in *God*. A beggar outside the temple asks for money in God's name—

because even he knows that people drop their logic when "God" is mentioned. But inside the temple? Bigger beggars sit. Dressed in robes, called "Purohits." They are not asking—they are *demanding*, manipulating, exploiting through fear.

They say you have *Kaal Sarp Dosh*, so you must buy a gemstone. They say you're cursed by *Rahu*, and 35 lakhs mantra jaap can save you. Twenty priests will chant. You will pay. Why? Because you're afraid. You're blind. You *believe*.

This is not spirituality. This is business. This is fear-driven exploitation.

Do not mistake this as a rejection of all belief. I'm not saying belief is inherently wrong. What I'm saying is—**fear makes belief blind**. And blind belief is dangerous.

History proves it: *Devadasi, Sati Pratha, animal sacrifice*, even *child sacrifice*—all were once "justified" by blind belief. These horrors were not born from evil alone—they were born from **unquestioned obedience**.

So I ask you: don't surrender your mind. Don't hand over your soul.

Be your own light. Like Buddha said: *"Appo Deepo Bhava"*—be a light unto yourself. Don't believe in me. Don't believe in anyone. Trust only what you have seen, felt, and known with your own heart.

Walk your own path. Think with your own mind. Feel with your own soul.

Because until you stop believing blindly, you will never truly live freely.

The Path of Realization: A Call to Live Authentically

According to me, when a newborn enters this world, we should not rush to assign them an identity—be it Hindu, Muslim, Sikh, Christian, or any other label. These identities are inherited, not chosen. Let the child grow with freedom, let them observe, question, and experience life. Let them choose, or choose nothing at all. Maybe in this freedom, they will discover a new way entirely—a path that belongs only to them. This is the essence of the "New World."

Don't blindly trust books either. Every book is written by a human being, not by some divine hand. Respect knowledge, yes—but don't surrender to it. Test it. Question it. Feel it. Experience it. Truth is not a second-hand story. You don't have to live based on someone else's perception. You are the creation of your own kind. You are a spark of consciousness, a unique soul. You must scratch your own itch, find your own way. That is the beginning of realization. That is the path of mindfulness.

To "scratch your own itch" means accepting the truth that your suffering is yours—created by you, and only you can end it. No one is coming to save you. Maybe you'll meet a teacher or a guru along the way—someone like Krishna, Buddha, Mahaveer, Kabir, or Jesus. They might show you a direction. They may offer you a pen or a paper, but remember—**you must write your own story**. You must ignite your own candle in the deep darkness of your being. No one else can do it for you.

Let me give you a living example: **Gautama Buddha**. Born a prince, he had every comfort imaginable. But despite the luxury, something within him felt empty. He saw suffering in the world and couldn't ignore it. That discomfort became the fire that pushed him to leave everything behind—his palace, his title, his family. He searched deeply, not by reading scriptures or following blindly, but by meditating, experimenting, failing, and trying again.

He didn't become a follower; he became a seeker. And in that deep seeking, he awakened.

But even Buddha said, "Be a light unto yourself." He never asked to be followed—only understood. His teaching was not a religion; it was a method. But today, people follow even him like a religion, forgetting his original message. That's what I want to avoid. That's what I want to shake people out of.

My intention is not to comfort you—but to disturb you. I want you to feel a little lost, a little shaken. Because in comfort, we become lazy, we exploit our own potential. Comfort becomes a trap. But discomfort—that's the beginning of transformation.

I know this path is not for everyone. It only begins when there is a deep inner dissatisfaction, a feeling of "this is not it." If you are happy with a routine life, this message might not reach you. But if you are in pain, if you are questioning, if you are hungry for truth—then you are ready.

We have all been suffering for a long time, but enough is enough. Now, it's time to dance with your soul, to embrace life with awareness. Live like a Yogi—not necessarily someone who does yoga on a mat—but someone who lives with awareness, purpose, and detachment. Don't be just an educated laborer, trapped in a system that trains you to survive, but never to live.

Choose the path of realization. That's the path of a true human being.

The Path of Realization – Step 1: Recognition of Suffering

Would You Be Born Again? A Soul's Question

Ask yourself a simple yet profound question:

"What if God asked your soul to take birth again on Earth in a new body?"

Don't consider whether you are in heaven or hell—remove those ideas. Just reflect on this life, your current experience on Earth.

If your answer comes as a clear **"Yes"**, that's beautiful. You are in alignment with your life and at peace with your existence.

But if your answer is **"No"** or **"Never again,"** then this is the first sign that you are **suffering** here, even if you haven't accepted it yet. This question becomes the mirror. It reflects back the reality of your inner world.

The Sadness Beneath the Surface

I have seen this suffering around me—in the corporate world, especially. I've seen people walking around with long faces, drained of spirit. Many live far from their families, facing daily challenges—bad food, loneliness, health issues, anxiety. I've seen people smoking, drinking—not out of joy, but to escape the pain of their lives.

From the outside, they may appear "fine" or "happy." But inside, they are hurting. Inside, they feel empty. And still, they continue doing the same work, the same routine.

Why?

Not because there is no other way. But because of one powerful force: **fear**.

The fear of the unknown.
The fear of change.
The fear of insecurity.
The fear of letting go.

They overthink the consequences and lose touch with their inner voice. But this fear has made them spiritually **impotent**—unable to move, even when their soul is screaming for something more.

The Rocket Analogy: Escape the System

Here, the metaphor of a rocket applies beautifully.

A rocket needs to generate enough energy to escape Earth's gravitational pull. In the same way, you too must **generate enough potential within yourself** to break free from the system that binds you.

To escape the matrix of fear and comfort, you must awaken your own inner fire.

And that energy comes from reconnecting with your soul—from remembering who you are and why you are here.

Discover the Inner World

You have your own world inside.

Dive into that space. There is always something waiting for you there—something sacred and pure. It could be your calling, your purpose, or your peace.

Just sit back. Relax. Stop the mind from running here and there. **Empty your cup**—clear your thoughts. Let the chatter fade.

Rest—deep, conscious rest—is the best medicine.

If you are suffering, or in pain, **surrender**. There's no shame in letting go for a while. Take time to **heal**.

And while you rest, ask yourself:

- *Do I want to continue living like this?*

- *What else is possible for me?*

- *What is the purpose of my life?*

Let your **subconscious mind** respond. It holds incredible wisdom. It will answer—not through logic, but through emotion, intuition, and inner signals.

The Dance of Mind, Heart, and Soul

When you receive an answer, don't believe it immediately. **Test it. Live it. Feel it.**

If your **mind**, **heart**, and **soul** begin to move in the same direction—if you feel peace, joy, and energy rising from within—**follow that.**

When everything inside you aligns, life becomes poetic.
That is when you discover the path of **love**.
Follow it blindly.

Don't Fear the Consequence

Now, let go of the fear of outcome.

Everybody must die someday. That is a fact. But how you live today, that is in your hands.

I don't follow success.
I don't chase any goal.
This work—this life—is what I love.
And I can live like this forever, without regret.

If death comes to me today, I will die smiling. Why?

Because I took the **first step of courage**.
I listened to my soul.

Surrender Like Krishna Taught

As Lord Krishna said in the **Bhagavad Gita**:

"Karma karo, phal ki chinta mat karo."
(Do your work, don't worry about the results.)

That is the essence of peace. Work from the heart, without attachment to the outcome. Let your actions be your offering.

The Journey Begins Here

This is the **first step** in the path of realization:
To recognize that you are suffering.

To ask yourself the right questions.
To sit in silence.
To reconnect with your inner self.

And once you do, the journey truly begins.
Not outward—but inward.

This is the life of the **Yogi**.
A life not of escape, but of **awareness**.

A life not driven by goals, but moved by **truth**.

The Fire Walk of Belief: A Reflection on Faith, Illusion, and Identity

In various spiritual and cultural traditions, individuals walk on embers, a ritual that might seem dangerous or irrational at first glance. However, beneath the surface, this act holds a symbolic meaning that transcends physical endurance. It is not merely the body that walks through the fire, but a deeper belief that walks with it—a belief that the body may burn, but the soul remains untouched. Firewalking, therefore, becomes an expression of the understanding that the body is transient and mortal, while the soul is eternal. It is a metaphorical journey reminding us that while the body may experience pain or even destruction, the true self remains beyond such harm.

This ritual serves another purpose too: it represents the burning away of desire—particularly lust. As individuals walk through fire, they are not only testing their faith, but also symbolically burning their worldly attachments. In this sense, fire becomes a purifier. Lust, which ties us to the illusion of permanence in the physical realm, is what truly burns. Letting go of it becomes an act of liberation. The fire is no longer a threat but a tool of transformation.

Similarly, there are practices where people place fire in their mouths. From an external viewpoint, this might appear to be madness. The rational mind questions the logic: why risk injury, why threaten your own ability to eat or speak for days? Yet, for the one who believes, it is an act of devotion, of strength, of transcendence. It reflects the self-respect that stems from unwavering faith. The believer doesn't need to know the scientific reason behind the act; the act itself is a manifestation of belief, and belief—when powerful—becomes its own justification.

This brings us to a deeper understanding of how belief operates within the human psyche. Those who know, act with clarity; those who do not know, may still act—but their experience will often be accompanied by confusion or pain. Yet all must act. In this lies a paradox: whether guided by knowledge or ignorance, human beings are driven to engage in rituals and behaviors that reflect their internal realities.

When a group comes together, belief often becomes collective. A phenomenon occurs where shared energy and intention shape individual experience. Consider the idea of being summoned or hypnotized into believing something false—such as being a dog. The mind, under suggestion, begins to accept this false identity and act accordingly. The person might bark, crawl, or behave in ways completely unaligned with their true nature. This is the power of belief—both beautiful and terrifying. It can liberate or deceive, elevate or reduce.

Faith, in its purest form, can lead one through fire unscathed. But blind faith, devoid of understanding, can also lead one into illusion. The line between belief and delusion is thin, and it is only through self-awareness that one can truly walk it. When knowledge dawns—when the individual realizes the truth of who they are—there is no longer any need for external demonstrations. Rituals lose their meaning once the inner realization is complete.

In conclusion, rituals like firewalking or fire-eating are more than just dramatic displays. They are reflections of deeper truths about the body, the soul, and the illusions that tie them together. They challenge us to examine what we believe, why we believe it, and whether our actions are guided by truth or illusion. And ultimately, they remind us that while the body may burn, the soul remains untouched—eternal, unchanging, and free.

The Hypnotism of Belief: A Journey from Illusion to Inner Awakening

Hypnotism is not limited to the realm of stage tricks or suggestive commands. It is a deeper phenomenon that subtly shapes our perceptions, behaviors, and even our identities. One might be hypnotized into believing they are a monkey— behaving and responding in ways alien to their true nature. Yet, this same hypnotism operates quietly in our daily lives. We are hypnotized by society, by traditions, by voices around us telling us what we are and how we should be.

Why does the average person—an "admin" of his life, rational and aware—still go to temples in search of God? Because even he is under the influence of this deeper hypnotism. Even if you remind him that God resides within, in the very core of his being, he will respond with skepticism. He will argue that everyone else may be misguided, but his actions are sensible. He cannot see that he too is pulled by the same invisible strings.

We approach God with expectations. We fast, not for purity, but with desires tightly packed in our prayers. Even during fasting, we cleverly find ways to indulge—sneaking in fruit-laden plates and sipping tea not twice but four times. Fasting, instead of being an act of transcendence, becomes just another modified indulgence. It is not the action, but the intention that reveals whether we are free or still bound.

If our faith is outward—attached to rituals, objects, or the approval of others—we remain trapped. Our soul remains confined in the illusion of the external. But if that same faith turns inward, it blossoms. It becomes meditation. It becomes yoga. It becomes true worship.

The real pilgrimage is not to a temple but into the self. And when we make that journey, we become watchers—like a yogi standing at the peak of a mountain. No longer concerned with being seen, but seeing all. No longer desperate to be understood, but understanding everything. In that solitude, in that height of self-awareness, there is no anxiety, no expectation. Just the joy of the wind, the serenity of the view, and the deep satisfaction of having arrived within.

This is freedom—not from the world, but from the hypnosis of needing the world to validate us.

<u>**Sutra - 2**</u>

The Solitary Truth of Existence

Alone in the Infinite

You are born alone.
You live alone.
And one day, you will die alone.

This is not a cruel twist of fate—this *is* the truth, the one truth the world tries so hard to forget. A truth buried beneath layers of distraction, of fleeting friendships, of hollow celebrations and temporary love stories. But I will not let it be forgotten. I want to teach you this, no matter how hard it is to hear. Because someone has to say it. Someone has to look the truth in the eye and not flinch.

I am alone in this entire universe.

Yes, you might hear that and feel a sting of sadness. A quiet ache. A whisper of despair. Because all the relationships we build, all the bonds we swear are unbreakable—they're not eternal. They are just a time pass. A beautiful, heartbreaking illusion we use to soften the sharp edges of our solitude.

We've been wandering alone through the infinite for longer than memory can hold. Before we had names. Before we had faces. Before this body, this voice, this brief flicker of existence—we were alone. Drifting through space and time, untethered. And now we wear masks, speak sweet words, hold hands in the dark. But deep down, we know: no one truly knows us. No one truly walks with us. Not all the way.

The laughter, the love, the pain—it all happens inside us. No one can crawl into your soul and carry your burdens. No one can die your death for you. The silence that awaits you at the end? It is yours alone.

But there is a strange kind of power in this truth. A terrifying freedom. If we accept that we are alone, utterly and completely, then nothing can shake us. We stop needing others to make us whole. We stop chasing permanence in a world built on dust and echoes. We become something more. Something unbreakable.

So yes—this life, this world, this dream—it is a solitary path. You can walk it with others for a while, but never forget: their footprints will fade. Only yours will remain.

And when it all falls silent, when the stars burn out and the sky forgets your name, you will remember: You were always alone.
And that's what made you infinite.

Loneliness and Solitude: A Dance of the Soul

The Yogi speaks—not with words, but with silence. And in that silence, he points towards a truth the world dares not speak of: **loneliness**.

Loneliness is not what it seems. It is not an absence—it is a presence. A presence of desire, of memory, of longing. Loneliness is the ego's most cunning weapon. It gnaws at you, whispers in the dark, makes you crave the noise of others. And when people feel lonely, they do what the ego wants—they rush to connect, to belong, to escape.

But solitude…
Solitude is different. Solitude is the death of the ego.
And so, it is its enemy.

Loneliness is born of the world—it is not the state of the soul. It is born when you *remember* someone, when you *miss* something, when your

heart searches for what is not present. It is full of
noise. It is full of shadows.

But solitude… solitude is peace. Solitude is silence.
Solitude is when the soul begins to awaken.
In solitude, there is no desire.
There is only *truth*.

Contemplation begins in solitude.
Realization *requires* it.

The soul… the soul is not the mind. It is not thought.
It is not name or form or memory. The soul does
not wear a veil because it has nothing to hide. It
does not fight to win—because it knows it *has
already won*. It is invincible. Immortal. Unshaken.
The soul needs no body. The soul *is* the beyond.

You will not see others… not truly… until you have
seen *yourself*.
You relate to this world because you still believe it
exists.
But one day, when the veil lifts, you will realize—
you relate to others not because they are real, but
because *you* still are.

This is the truth: **"I" exists only because "you" exist.**
"I" and "you" are twins—bound, born together.

If there are people, then there can be a king.
But if there are no people—what is a king? A ghost in a crown.

So long as others exist in your mind, *you* will exist.
And so long as "I" exists... you will never know solitude.

Loneliness will haunt you. It will drag you into the depths of despair.
It will whisper falsehoods. It will chain you to the wheel of life and death.

But solitude?
Solitude will break those chains.
Solitude will show you that *you were never the body, never the name, never the sorrow*.

Solitude is not an escape—it is a return.
To the soul. To silence.
To that which cannot be born, and cannot die.

The Dance of Opposites: Why Life Needs Both Light and Shadow

Keep this in mind—engrave it into the walls of your heart: for life to be *complete*, both the **soul** and the **ego** are necessary. As strange as it sounds, they are not enemies—they are **complementary** forces, two sides of the same eternal coin. Without one, the other has no meaning. Without one, life loses its shape, its contrast, its flavor.

If there is no **ego**, no sense of "I," then you will never come to know the soul. The ego builds the wall, yes—but without the wall, how would you ever learn to break it down? How would you learn transcendence without first being trapped? The ego creates the illusion, but the soul awakens when the illusion is seen for what it is. That is its purpose.

Think of **sorrow**. If sorrow never touched you— how would you ever recognize **happiness**? You would smile, but not know the worth of that smile. You would laugh, but never from the heart. It is *because* you have cried in the night that the morning light feels warm on your face.

If you have never burned with **anger**, how would you even begin to understand **peace**? Peace is not just the absence of noise—it is the cooling after the storm. The stillness that arrives *after* the thunder has passed. True peace is known only by those who have trembled with fury and chosen to lay it down.

And what of **fear**? Without fear, what is **courage**? Courage is not the absence of fear—it is the defiance of it. It is the moment you step forward even as your knees shake. The soldier who marches into the battlefield. The child who speaks the truth in a room full of judgment. The artist who bares their soul to a world that may not understand. *That* is courage. Born from fear, shaped by it, made meaningful through it.

In the same way—without a **friend**, could you ever know what it means to have an **enemy**? Without love, would betrayal matter? Without attachment, could loss exist? Every emotion, every experience gains its depth from its opposite.

Let me give you a real example. Imagine a man who has lived a perfect life—no sorrow, no loss, no failure. Everything he touches turns to gold. But one day, he stands at the funeral of someone he never expected to lose. And for the first time, he feels **emptiness**. In that moment, his whole life rewrites itself. The smiles were real—but now, he understands *why* they mattered. Because now he knows what it means to lose.

This is the truth: if there is **life**, there must be **death**. If there is day, night must follow. If there is joy, sorrow is its silent twin. It is this dance between opposites that makes life *alive*. Remove one, and the dance ends. The song falls silent. The journey halts.

And so, let it be understood: your soul needs your ego, just as the flame needs the night to be seen. Your sorrow gives birth to your wisdom. Your fear opens the door to your bravery. This life, with all its contradictions, is not broken—it is perfectly designed.

Without the bitter, the sweet is meaningless.
Without the fall, the rise is weightless.
Without death... life loses all its urgency.

Let every emotion, every experience, every shadow and every spark be part of your story.
Only then will the journey be whole.
Only then will the soul rise from within the storm—
not untouched by life, but shaped by it.

The Grand Illusion: Arrogance and the Forgotten Soul

Arrogance makes you animal.
The soul makes you divine.
And between these two lies the tragedy of mankind.

Arrogance is not just pride. It is not just superiority. It is a **trickster**—a shapeshifter cloaked in your own intelligence. It doesn't come from outside. No, it *rises from within*, and worse, it uses your own intellect against you. Your logic. Your brilliance. Your sharp tongue and even sharper thoughts— **these are its weapons**.

Understand this clearly: **arrogance works through the mind**. Its illusion is not in the body—it's in the thinking. It tells you you're right. It tells you you're wise. It makes you feel chosen, enlightened, better than others, while it quietly **separates you from your own soul**.

And what has it done to the world?

Look outside. Look carefully.

People roam the streets with God on their lips, gods in their hands, idols in every corner, and scriptures in every home. Temples shine. Statues are bathed in milk and gold. Prayers rise like smoke every morning—and yet the world burns.

Do you see it?

In worship itself, love has been destroyed.
In prayer, the path to the soul has been closed. Because arrogance has done something devastating—it has turned your eyes *outward*.

It has **placed God outside of you**.

And now that you think truth is in the temple, why would you ever search within? Why would you ever sit in silence when there's so much ceremony to perform? Why would you go inward, when you've been told the divine lives in stone, not in your breath?

And so you worship.
You repeat the rituals.
You bow to forms while forgetting the formless.

And all the while, arrogance stands behind the curtains of religion—**and it laughs**.

It watches as people kill each other in the name of peace.
It watches as nations burn for the sake of sacred names.
It watches blood spilled on the soil that once sang the songs of sages.

And it smiles. Because this is its masterpiece.

Arrogance does not care which god you worship— so long as you think *only* you are right.
It does not care what truth you speak—so long as you never *live* it.

This is the web it has spun. A web so subtle, so intelligent, that you never even feel the threads around your soul. It has bound you not with chains, but with thoughts. With pride. With knowledge turned toxic.

This is its greatest victory: it has made you forget that **God was never outside**.
That **truth was always within**.
That **your soul is not found in books, but in silence**.

But if even once you sit... truly sit... in stillness—not with borrowed beliefs, but with raw presence—you will see what arrogance fears most:

You are divine.
You were always divine.
And you don't need to fight to prove it.

When that knowing rises, the illusion shatters.
And arrogance? It cannot survive in the light of the soul.

The Ego's Final Disappearance: A Silent Truth of Life

Catching the ego is like trying to catch the mind itself—impossible with the same tools it uses to deceive you. It is a phantom wearing your voice, hiding behind your name, speaking your language so well that you begin to think *it is you*. And this is its greatest power: **it fools you without you ever knowing**.

Your whole life, the ego walks beside you like a shadow that never leaves. It guides your decisions, colors your emotions, wears your victories like medals, and blames others for your defeats. It builds stories around your identity, constantly whispering: *"This is who you are."* And you believe it. Why wouldn't you? It feels natural. It feels right.

But ego is not your truth.
It is your prison.

And the cruelest trick? It abandons you when you need it most.

At the moment of death—when everything you knew begins to dissolve—the ego suddenly steps aside. Not out of kindness, but because it has no use anymore. It can't survive what's coming. It cannot follow the soul beyond the final breath. Its job is done.

And in that moment, something extraordinary happens.

For one or two seconds, just before death, a person becomes completely calm.

You can see it in their eyes. You can feel it in the room. The struggle ends, the noise fades, and all that's left is a deep, inexplicable stillness.

That stillness is not fear. It's not pain.
It is the **soul taking over the body**, fully and without resistance—for the first time since birth.
All the illusions the ego built, all the false identities, the pride, the stories—it all vanishes.
And what remains is the purest truth of existence: just **being**.

Let me give you a real example.

An old man lies in a hospital bed. For years, he argued, boasted, chased success, built walls around his heart. He had answers for everything. Control was his comfort. Ego was his god.

But now, in his final hour, all that falls away.
His breathing slows.
His eyes stop searching.
And then, for a brief, beautiful moment... there is peace.
Not the kind of peace that comes from comfort—but the kind that comes from **truth**.
In that instant, it is as if his soul says, *"Finally, now that the ego has stepped away, I can return."*

And it does.

This moment—this surrender—is what makes life
beautiful, and heartbreaking.
Because it shows us how close we were to the truth
the entire time.
But we were busy being someone. Busy proving
something.
Busy chasing what the ego promised, while the soul
waited silently.

The ego took you only up to your head—filled it
with noise, knowledge, pride.
But it never let you wake up.
It never let you go inward, to the heart, to the self.
And because of that, **Brahma—the absolute
truth—remained hidden**.

But even so, life has a strange mercy.
It lets the soul return at the end.
And in that return, even for a fleeting second, you
become what you always were.

That...
That is the secret beauty of life.

**The Vanishing Point of the Soul: An Essay on Truth,
Ego, and Illusion**

In the silent realm of the soul, everything known vanishes. Words collapse, thoughts dissolve, and identity—the "I"—ceases to exist. It is here, in this vanishing point, that the soul begins. Yet, ironically, whatever we try to say about it becomes arrogance, because language itself is a construct of the ego. Any description is bound to fail, for the soul cannot be captured by thought or spoken word. At best, one can only hint, gesture, or point toward it. The rest must be discovered by the seeker through experience, through *sadhana*.

The Nature of Arrogance and the Silent Soul

Arrogance is the assertion of "I" — the self that claims to know, to own, to be something separate. The soul, on the other hand, is that which remains when this "I" disappears. When the mind is without thought, when there is no self trying to control or name the experience — that is where the soul exists. It is not something you can look at with your physical eyes. You must look with inner vision, which opens only through deep spiritual practice.

For example, in a moment of deep meditation, when one forgets the body, forgets the identity, and simply *is*, something beyond the ordinary is felt. Not heard, not seen — just *known* in a way that bypasses the intellect. This is not arrogance; this is surrender.

Fear, Darkness, and the Resistance to the Soul

Fear is the guardian of the illusion. It is fear that prevents people from going deeper, from letting go of identity, relationships, desires, and pain. Fear will not allow you to die to your false self while you are still alive. But this death — the death of ego — is essential for knowing the soul.

This is why spiritual masters like Buddha and Mahavira went into the forest. They renounced everything — not because the world was bad, but because the world was loud. They sought silence. They meditated not to escape, but to enter a new reality. Through deep meditation, Buddha attained *Nirvana*, the blowing out of the ego's flame. Mahavira reached *Kevalya*, pure knowledge beyond duality. They gave different names to the same experience — the absolute truth.

How the World Twists the Truth

Yet, the world did not understand them. It rarely does. What began as pure truth became doctrine. What began as a revolution of spirit became religion. Their words were taken, twisted by fear and power, and made into organized systems that often contradict the very essence of what they taught.

Take Jesus, for instance. He spoke of the Kingdom of God *within*. He lived simply, taught love, forgiveness, and oneness with the divine. But fear and power could not let this message spread freely. He was crucified. And after his death, the same system that feared him turned him into an icon — a God to be worshipped externally, rather than a state of being to be realized internally.

control Thus was born Christianity — not necessarily as Jesus intended, but as the world could tolerate. The inner truth was turned outward, and the soul's whisper was turned into dogma. This is the nature of illusion. The truth, when it becomes fear's hostage, is transformed into a tool of.

The Call to Sadhana: Becoming Zero

To return to the truth, one must go back within. *Sadhana* — the spiritual path — requires becoming zero. This means dropping all identities, all stories, all attachments. Not in hatred or repression, but in deep surrender. The soul is not something you acquire; it is what you uncover when everything else falls away.

A modern example could be seen in mystics like Ramana Maharshi, who sat silently on the Arunachala mountain, teaching seekers to ask the question: "Who am I?" He never gave long sermons, but his silence was louder than any speech. In that silence, many experienced the same truth that Buddha and Jesus spoke of — a truth without name, without form, without arrogance

Seeing Without Eyes

Truth cannot be told — it can only be *lived*. The soul cannot be shown — it can only be *realized*. The world outside will always show you a version of God that suits its fear. But the real journey is inward, where no thought lives, where no self exists. That is where the soul waits — not to be found, but to be remembered.

You must not look with eyes, but with presence. You must not speak with tongue, but with silence. And you must not seek to gain the soul, but to *lose* everything that covers it. Then, what remains is not you — but the truth itself.

(Buddha said that the truth is inside you do not seek for outer world When buddha tell the truth to

the world "Samsaar", Samsaar means EGO (the outer world) but the ego (The darkness) drowned all the truth onto itself. Not only it swallowed the truth of buddha but also twisted it with the deception and present it to you. This is what happens when darkness is heard as the truth. If you make him understand the truth, it will make you the truth and worship you and after making you God, it will take everyone out. "MAHANKAAR" will show the truth outside, he will show God outside, this is illusion. Jesus is the biggest example of this. He too was killed by the evil (MAHANKAAR) spirit, then he was made God and brought outside and converted into Christianity.)

THE MAHANKAAR-EGO

I call it "Mahankaar", Buddha had called it "Mara". Now the question is how to reach there, now whatever I will tell you, it will be swallowed by "Mahankaar", so now you will have to find it yourself, I can only tell you this that if you will not find anything outside, you will find it, everything is inside.

"Mahankaar" is very powerful and it is very illusory and like the soul it is everywhere and immortal. You will not be able to defeat it directly. For this either a great Guru is needed or it is possible that God himself comes into you. I am giving a little indication of its power. If you take your name then understand this. And if you become silent then you will see it immediately. It will immediately come into your silent thoughts. You understand this; you cannot defeat it with your thinking. (This cannot be defeated, this is my indication that this cannot be defeated) Just recognize this, understand this, all the sins and all the pain, all the suffering is nowhere to be found, it is all within you. Don't go far from yourself.

There is no war in the city, there is no peace anywhere in the city and there is no God outside. Outside is just a reflection of the world inside. Whatever storm there is inside, it also rages outside. If there is peace inside, you will not find the glimpse of the storm anywhere outside.

The Thorned Crown: The Illusion of "I" and "Mine" as the Root of Sorrow

In the grand theatre of life, there exists a subtle yet powerful illusion that governs almost every action, every desire, and every sorrow: the illusion of "I" and "mine." These two small words — so deeply embedded in our identity — are the seeds of endless suffering. When a person says "this is mine," or "I am this," a chain of consequences begins that pulls them deeper into the world of attachment, conflict, and restlessness.

Nowhere is this more visible than in the story of a king — a symbol of ultimate worldly success, yet often the most restless and tormented figure in his own kingdom.

The Path to Power: A Trail of Violence and Karma

A king does not simply become a king. His path to the throne is usually paved with blood. To claim power, he must destroy others who also desired it — competitors, enemies, former friends. He may kill a thousand to become sovereign, but those thousand souls do not leave him in peace. If not literally, then in memory, in guilt, in karma — they haunt him.

This is why it is said that the **crown of a king is made of thorns**. It appears glorious, but it carries with it the sharp pain of all that had to be lost, broken, and destroyed to wear it. The king may hold the crown, but he also holds responsibility for every drop of blood spilled for it.

And the irony? Even after becoming king, peace does not arrive. The fear of losing the throne begins. Enemies multiply. New wars begin. Insecurity sets in. To protect what is "mine," he must go on killing, controlling, manipulating. The cycle continues endlessly — a loop of fear, pride, and violence, all to protect an identity that was never truly his to begin with.

The Burden of "I" and "Mine"

This king is not just a historical figure — he lives in all of us.

We may not rule empires, but we all build kingdoms: a job title, a relationship, a house, an image, a reputation. And once we say *"this is mine"* or *"I am this,"* we begin defending it with all our energy. We lie for it, fight for it, suffer for it — and if threatened, we're even willing to hurt others or ourselves for it.

But all of this begins with a false premise: that we are separate, that something can be owned, that identity is fixed. The truth is — everything in life is temporary. Nothing is truly ours. Not the body, not the name, not even the thoughts. Clinging to what we think is "ours" only multiplies sorrow.

Freedom Lies in Surrender

The great spiritual masters realized this. Buddha left his kingdom not to become poor, but to become free. Mahavira dropped every possession to realize that the soul is beyond name and form. Jesus said, *"Blessed are the meek, for they shall inherit the earth,"* pointing toward humility, not conquest.

True kingship is not ruling others, but ruling oneself. And that can only happen when the "I" and "mine" dissolve. Only in that emptiness — free from possession, identity, and ego — does peace arrive.

" Yeh Jaag mayli maya, swapn me mujhe nahawaye ,, na hi paya tazgi ar sadhu sugandh bhi khoye."

Shubham Sasvath

Means:-

Yes, this world is *Maya* — an illusion. But what makes Maya so powerful is that it doesn't just deceive through obvious things like materialism, greed, or pleasure. It also hides inside spirituality. You can meditate with ego. You can chant mantras with pride. You can take a dip in the Ganges believing you are purifying your soul — and yet, that very belief may be strengthening the illusion, not breaking it.

As I said:

"...I got the illusion that I would purify myself by taking a bath in the Ganges..."

It's like waking up inside a dream and realizing you're still dreaming. Even the so-called *remedies* can become traps if they come from the wrong place — from the ego, from fear, from a desire to "achieve" something spiritually.

The True Prayer: The Inner Journey of the Soul

In a world consumed by noise, rituals, and outward performance, we often forget that the **soul does not speak in noise.** It speaks in silence. True purification, real peace, and the journey of liberation do not lie outside — they are within. The mistake of humanity, repeated through generations, is the belief that salvation lies in actions done outside, in places we visit, or in practices we perform without presence.

But **the purification of the soul** can only happen through **true prayer** — and **true prayer** does not come from the lips, but from the **heart's surrender** and the **soul's cry**.

The Illusion of the Outside World

You may bathe in the holiest rivers, visit the most sacred temples, light countless lamps and chant a thousand names — but if the heart is still holding ego, anger, pride, and regret, then these rituals only add to the **burden**, not remove it. The outer world is heavy. Every action driven by appearance, by pride, or by guilt without transformation only **tightens the chains of suffering**.

It is only when one turns inward, sits in silence, and begins to speak with their own soul, that **the real prayer begins**.

The Moment of Realization

There comes a moment in every seeker's life — a quiet but powerful shift — when they pause and ask themselves, *"Was the path I was walking truly mine? Or was I lost in the illusion?"* And if the answer comes — not from the mind but from the **soul** — then that is the beginning of a real spiritual journey.

That voice from within — even if it only whispers — is the most sacred moment of one's life. It is **Grace**.

When the soul says, *"You were wrong, but now you can begin again,"* you are born again — not in body, but in consciousness.

That is **prayer**. That is **realization**. That is **salvation**.

The Birth of a Yogi

From this inner awakening, the **Yogi is born**. Not the one who performs postures or wears robes, but the one who has renounced the outside path for the inner one. The one who has stopped running behind the world and started walking into the self. A true Yogi is not someone who escapes life, but someone who faces the self with truth and chooses the soul above all.

To **worship the soul** is to become a Yogi — because the soul is the purest temple, the final teacher, and the truest God.

This Earthly Life and the Pain of Return

Even today, when I ask myself, *"Do I want to be born again on this earth?"* the answer comes from the depths of my being — *"What will I do come here again?"*

This is not depression. This is not despair. This is the pain of a soul that has seen enough illusion, that has suffered enough through lifetimes of forgetfulness. It is the cry of a being who remembers that this world, unless lived with awareness, is a cycle of suffering.

And yet, I am still here — which means the journey is not over. The soul is still calling, and I must walk. Not toward the outside, but toward the inside.

The Wound That Never Heals: A Journey Through Love, Trust, and the Illusion of Permanence

There will come a day when the answer to this question will change. But for now, when I look around and within, I see a reflection of the same sin, the same evil, mirrored in everyone—and in myself. The deception I've encountered outside is mirrored by the deceiver that lies within me. At the heart of all of this is fear—a primal, gripping fear that someone might do something to me that I do not want. This discomfort festers, and in its shadow, neither love nor trust can survive.

Love and trust—beautiful as they are—are also the most dangerous forces in a person's life. They make us vulnerable. They soften our walls. They make us human—and weak. A man does not need to be attacked to be destroyed. Just take love and trust from him, and he will slowly begin to decay from within. This is how sin begins: not with a knife or a lie, but with the invisible, lasting wound of betrayed trust and shattered love.

The Eternal Wound

The pain inflicted by swords or bullets can heal. The scars may fade over time. But the wounds of love and trust—those do not heal. They linger. They fester. They remain alive like a wound that never dries. And to avoid being wounded again, man begins to wound others. He builds walls, masks, weapons—not to hurt others first, but to not be hurt again. And so, the cycle of hurt becomes the chain of hatred.

Where there is love, there will always be the potential for hate. Where there is trust, betrayal lurks nearby. These opposites are born from each other and are bound together like day and night. The greater the love, the more painful the hatred. The deeper the trust, the more devastating the betrayal.

The Middle Path

Thus, arises the question: what is the way out of this cycle?

The answer lies in the middle path. To love without attachment. To care without expecting. One can love a tree, a mountain, or a sunset—there is no betrayal in such love. Why? Because there is no expectation from it. This is a love that liberates, not binds. True love does not say, *"You belong to me."* It says, *"You are free, and I still love you."*

This can only be understood when we recognize two cosmic laws. The first is the **law of impermanence**—everything in the external world changes, dies, transforms. And the second is the **law of permanence within**—your soul, your true self, is eternal. Real love can only bloom when we grasp both. Until one reaches this state of awareness, all forms of love are temporary—they rise intensely but fall just as fast.

A Live Example: Raghav's Journey

Let us take a real-world example—Raghav, a young man full of hope, once trusted a childhood friend, Aarav, more than anyone. They built dreams together, shared secrets, and believed that their bond was unbreakable. But time and ambition drifted Aarav into a world of selfish gains. One day, he betrayed Raghav by stealing an opportunity they were supposed to share—a business venture built on mutual trust.

For Raghav, this betrayal wasn't just financial—it was spiritual. He felt something inside him die. It wasn't anger that consumed him at first, but a cold emptiness. In the months that followed, Raghav stopped trusting others. He withdrew, built walls around himself, and started suspecting love itself.

But years later, after a long period of introspection and pain, he met a Buddhist teacher who taught him the essence of *non-attachment*. The teacher said, "You suffered because your love had expectations. You gave it the form of ownership. You made trust a contract."

That line shattered something inside Raghav—and built something new.

He began to meditate, reflect, and slowly understand the transient nature of the world. He began to love again—not for gain, not with fear, but with awareness. He let go of the poison of betrayal and realized the truth: that the soul is not here to be protected from pain, but to grow through it.

The Path Within

Eventually, we all come to the gates of self-realization. When we turn inward, the soul begins to whisper truths we were not ready to hear. Our old world begins to crumble—our illusions, our identities, even our relationships. It's terrifying. We may want to run back to the comfort of illusion. But if we stay, if we endure, we find something deeper.

We realize that love is not possession, trust is not dependency, and pain is not the end. These are steps—necessary steps—toward liberation. And so, the next time you are betrayed or broken, do not close your heart. Instead, open it so wide that even betrayal gets dissolved in your understanding.

The answer will change. But only when **you** change.

The Final Question: Who Am I?

A Journey from Illusion to Realization

When everything is stripped away—when the external battles are over, the ambitions fall silent, and the illusions begin to dissolve—then arises the most fundamental and terrifying question a human being can ever ask: **Who am I?**

This question is not just philosophical. It is not merely poetic. It is existential. Because whoever you think you are today—your name, status, roles, achievements—will eventually disappear. This identity you wear so proudly is only temporary. And when it is gone, what will remain?

The Silence After the Storm

For some, this question never arises. They stay entangled in the noise of the world, running from one illusion to another. But for the seeker— someone who has begun to see through the veil— this question becomes unavoidable. And the moment this question takes root, your real journey begins.

The answer to "Who am I?" is different for everyone, because the journey is personal. But if you ever reach a point where this answer becomes one and the same—beyond form, beyond thought, beyond language—then you have touched the edge of truth. That is **Realization**. That is the beginning of the **path of the Yogi**.

From this point forward, the **battle with the outside world ends**, and the **inner battle begins**— and this inner battle is infinitely more complex.

The Price of God

Getting to God, to truth, to the essence of being— is not a joke. It is not a hobby or a weekend retreat.

God is very expensive. Not in wealth, but in sacrifice. You will have to give up everything: your illusions, your comforts, your beliefs, your very sense of self.

If you understand this, you are wise. If you do not, you will remain trapped in the very illusion that promises freedom.

Look at the lives of those who sought truth deeply—**Swami Vivekananda**, for instance. He was a giant in the realm of thought, a restless seeker of knowledge. But even he, in his brilliance, created a different world—a mental construct so large that it consumed him. He did not become truly "knowledgeable" in the spiritual sense, because the trap of the intellect is subtle. Knowledge can become another form of ego, another prison.

And then there is **Dhyan**, a man overwhelmed by knowledge—so much so that his brain became a battlefield. His internal stress was so intense that it damaged his physical body. He couldn't sleep. He suffered deeply. This is the consequence of excessive intellectualism. The mind and the body are not separate—when one suffers, the other follows.

The Wisdom of Knowing You Know Nothing

In this light, **true wisdom**—true *Gyan*—is
something very different from accumulation. A real
Gyani is not the one who flaunts their knowledge,
but the one who says with complete humility: *"I am
a fool."*

Only a truly wise person can say this, because only
they understand the vastness of what they do not
know. The one who has tasted the ocean of truth
knows that no amount of learning can ever be
enough. The more you know, the more you realize
how little you know.

This is not pessimism—it is liberation. The mind no
longer needs to chase and prove. It becomes still. It
surrenders.

The Formula of Knowledge

So what is the **formula of knowledge**?
It is this:

**"The wise man knows he is a fool; the fool
believes he is wise."**

This paradox is the cornerstone of realization.
When you can look at yourself and say, *"I know
nothing"*, without shame or fear, then you are
ready for truth to unfold.

Conclusion: The Journey Within

The journey to self-realization is not a straight line. It is a spiral, a circle, a constant unfolding. The world outside may tempt you with its pleasures, illusions, and distractions, but once the real question—**"Who am I?"**—has been asked with honesty, there is no turning back.

You will lose much—comfort, identity, attachment—but you will gain something priceless: clarity.
Not answers, but **understanding**.
Not more knowledge, but **freedom from needing it**.

And that, finally, is the essence of being a Yogi.
Not one who escapes the world, but one who sees it clearly, walks through it mindfully, and knows that behind every answer... waits another question.

It is not that Shiv can be attained through the soul; the soul itself is Shiva: the true truth.

This is my second Sutra: Do not afraid to be alone, because you already alone. The samsara (the outer world) wants you to be engaged within it. System can't risk you to leave you free. People may around you can't see you alone but happy which is called solitude, they always drag you down to their level.

Suppose you have a bestfriend which is very close to you, you have shared everything of your life. You don't even realize that but a invisible bond you have created, your so called best friend can manipulate you, all of your decision of life. And things you will also follow. Your best friend also is your best enemy at the instance when he become best friend because he know everything about you. You can also in a pressure to acknowledge him every time.

Just believe on yourself you can be your best friend, Once you can enjoy solitude, you need no one you are enough. I want to tell you here that stand alone don't let the fear overcome you, you are alone enough to make a dent on the world or on the system. Just believe in yourself, even if you are in darkness of hell, even if you are dragging in your career just believe on you. This will give you the ultimate suffering for the first but also you gain ultimate experience of life, you raise as ultimate human.

In solitude you will learn to control your emotion, you will learn the focus. Alone means not to go Himalaya and meditate no.

Live like oil on water.

Don't let anyone to play with your emotion, feeling and life. You are absolute free from the birth. This is the second step of courage.

The Limitations of Labelling: Mistaking the Finger for the Moon

In the realm of human understanding, language is both a tool and a trap. One of the subtlest ways this trap manifests is through the act of labeling — assigning names, categories, and definitions to people, experiences, beliefs, and phenomena. While labels help us navigate the world, they also confine our perception. When we become too attached to these mental tags, we lose sight of the deeper reality they point toward.

Buddha offered a powerful metaphor to illustrate this point: **"My teaching is like a finger pointing to the moon. Do not mistake the finger for the moon."** This deceptively simple statement reveals a profound truth. The teachings, words, and concepts — even the sacred doctrines — are not the ultimate reality. They are indicators, tools meant to guide the seeker toward direct experience. To cling to the label or teaching as if it were the truth itself is to remain caught in illusion.

The Nature of Labels

Labeling often arises from the mind's need to simplify. It places the richness of reality into tidy boxes. A person becomes "good" or "bad," a religion becomes "true" or "false," an experience becomes "success" or "failure." These binary classifications distort the complexity of life. Worse, once a label is applied, it tends to solidify, reducing a dynamic reality to a static image. This prevents open inquiry, deeper understanding, and authentic connection.

For example, someone might hear the word "Buddhism" and immediately think of monks, temples, or meditation. But such images are just cultural representations — fingers pointing to the moon. If one gets stuck in these associations, one might never explore the living spirit of the Buddha's message, which is about awakening from suffering and seeing reality as it is.

A Real-Life Example

Consider the story of a woman named Aisha, who was born into a devout religious family. From a young age, she was taught that only her tradition was valid and that other paths were dangerous or misguided. Labels like "infidel," "heretic," or "enlightened" were commonly used in her community to classify outsiders or saints. But as Aisha grew older, she developed a deep curiosity about the world. She started reading sacred texts from other traditions — the Tao Te Ching, the Bhagavad Gita, the Gospels — and noticed something strange. Despite the different words, rituals, and symbols, many teachings pointed to the same truths: compassion, inner stillness, ego-transcendence, love.

Confused, she asked a visiting teacher, "How can all these paths claim to be the truth?" The teacher smiled and replied with the Buddha's metaphor: "Each tradition is like a finger pointing to the moon. But you must look beyond the finger to see what they're all pointing to."

It was then that Aisha realized she had been mistaking labels for truth. The labels had given her a false sense of certainty but had blocked her from experiencing the vastness of spiritual reality. She began to see the teachings not as competing claims, but as different languages pointing to the same silent, luminous awareness.

Beyond the Finger

Buddha's statement is not merely a critique of dogma, but a challenge to go deeper. It invites us to look beyond the surface — beyond words, categories, ideologies — and encounter truth directly. This applies not just to spiritual teachings but to everyday life.

When you call someone "a failure," are you seeing the whole person or just a concept? When you label yourself as "anxious," are you observing the emotion or becoming the emotion? When we step beyond labels, we encounter reality as it is — raw, living, and infinitely nuanced.

Labelling is useful only as a signpost, not as a destination. As soon as we take the signpost for the journey itself, we become lost in maps rather than walking the path. Buddha's metaphor serves as a timeless reminder: do not get caught in the forms, symbols, or doctrines. Use them — but then go beyond them. Look at the moon, not the finger.

In doing so, we awaken to a reality that cannot be named but only lived.

Mistaking the Vessel for the Elixir: How Stories, Labels, and Forms Obscure the Truth

In every age, great masters have appeared not to impose rigid doctrines, but to awaken human beings from illusion. Whether it was Krishna on the battlefield of Kurukshetra, Buddha beneath the Bodhi tree, or Jesus on the mountaintop — each pointed toward a truth that cannot be confined within words, stories, or forms. And yet, paradoxically, every time a master speaks, writes, or moves among people, his essence becomes reduced to scripture, myth, or ritual. What was meant to be a door becomes a wall. What was intended as a mirror becomes an idol.

The Trap of Literalism: When Symbols Become Snares

You cannot explain truth to all people with the same words. The truth must bend like a river to reach each soul. But humanity, in its obsession with certainty, grabs onto the words and forgets what they were pointing to.

In Hinduism, for instance, stories of gods and divine play — Krishna's leelas with Radha, Shiva's tandava, Rama's exile — were never meant as historical events to worship blindly. They were encoded symbols, profound metaphors for cosmic forces and inner states of being. Krishna was never merely a flute-playing boy; he was *Sat-Chit-Ananda* — existence, consciousness, and bliss. But what has happened over time? People have fallen in love with the **body of Krishna**, with the *Thakurji* idols, the garments, the rituals — and forgotten the **Saar** (essence) of what he said in the Bhagavad Gita.

Consider this verse:

"You have the right to perform your duty, but not to the fruits thereof."
(Bhagavad Gita 2.47)

This is not religious instruction — it is a universal insight into karma and detachment. But instead of internalizing this truth, many get lost in the stories of Radha-Krishna romance or temple ceremonies, mistaking the **Katha** (story) for the **Tatva** (essence). The metaphor was a raft to cross the river — not a relic to be worshiped while drowning.

A Living Example: The Man Who Worshipped the Frame

There once was a man who received a beautiful photo frame with an image of a mountain sunset. It was a gift from a traveler who had seen the actual mountain. The traveler told him, "This mountain is real, and standing on its peak will change you forever."

But the man fell in love with the frame. He polished it daily, bowed before it, built a temple around it — yet never once set out to find the mountain. When others came and asked what the mountain was like, he said, "Look at the frame! Isn't it divine?"

Such is what we do with truth. Instead of climbing toward the experience, we remain entangled in the pictures and poems that were meant to *inspire* us, not *define* us.

The Division of Dharma: The Case of Buddhism

The Buddha spoke nothing but clarity — and yet even clarity, once fossilized, can divide people. Only 140 years after his passing, Buddhism split into Theravāda and Mahāyāna — the "lesser" and the "greater" vehicles. The irony? Buddha never claimed a religion. He taught a way of seeing, of being, of awakening. But his words, like the finger pointing to the moon, became subjects of intellectual debate. One group emphasized monastic discipline and direct realization; the other sought to include laypeople and bodhisattva ideals. Both aimed to preserve the truth — and both ended up codifying it.

Why did this happen? Because even the purest teachings are filtered through the limitations of the human mind. Time changes, context changes, language evolves — but the interpretations often remain static. People do not adjust the vessel for the new generation; they serve the old wine in a cracked pot.

The Need to Renew the Language of Truth

Truth is timeless, but its **expression must be timely**. A river is eternal only if it flows. If it becomes stagnant, it turns into a swamp. The same applies to spiritual wisdom. If the meaning isn't reinterpreted, re-felt, and re-lived in each era, people will continue to drown in the words and miss the water.

This is why Krishna says in the Gita:

"Whenever there is a decline in righteousness, I manifest Myself."
(Bhagavad Gita 4.7)

But what does "manifest" mean? Is Krishna reborn with a peacock feather each time? No — it means truth *resurrects* in new forms, in new voices, in new seekers who are willing to see beyond labels, beyond forms, and touch the living flame of wisdom.

Reclaiming the Saar

The true seeker must constantly ask: **Am I seeing the moon, or still staring at the finger?** Am I holding onto stories because they comfort me, or am I diving into the raw, living truth they point to? The stories were always meant to help us — but if we do not grow beyond them, they become our prison.

Let us not dissolve into the physical forms of gods and idols. Let us not be trapped by the echo of the master's voice, forgetting to listen for the silence he spoke from. Let us change the language of truth with the times — not to dilute it, but to keep it alive.

Because truth cannot be inherited.
It must be rediscovered. Again. And again. And again.

The Illusion of Knowing: How Labeling Conceals Reality

We live in a world of names, categories, and definitions. Everything we encounter, we instantly label — and in doing so, we believe we understand it. But does labeling something truly mean we know it? Or are we merely arranging surfaces while the depth remains untouched?

Take the simple example of a tree. The moment we see it, our mind says, "That is a tree." And in that moment, we stop seeing. The label becomes the limit. The mystery is closed under a name.

But what is a tree, really?

On a superficial level, we describe its visible structure — trunk, leaves, branches, roots. Digging deeper, we describe its function — it produces oxygen, it participates in the ecosystem, it provides shelter, shade, and fruits. Go further still, and science tells us about its cellular makeup, its DNA, its ability to photosynthesize, and its evolutionary history.

Then we begin to specialize: *this* is a Neem tree. It has antiseptic properties. It's bitter in taste. It's used in traditional medicine, in Ayurveda, in toothpaste, and insect repellents. We can write hundreds of pages — about its origin, geographical spread, medical uses, pests that affect it, classifications of those pests, environmental value, cultural significance.

We begin to feel proud of this knowledge, even authoritative.

But then comes the real question:
Can we create a Neem tree?
Can we produce a new seed, from nothing?
Can we give birth to life itself?

The answer is no.

We can plant, we can modify, we can even clone —
but we cannot create the first principle of life. We
observe, we label, we study, and we use. But we do
not *know* in the truest sense. Our understanding is
not complete — it is functional. It is like reading a
poem in a foreign language using a dictionary. You
may understand the words, but the soul of the
poem is lost.

Labeling: The Comfort of Control

Labeling is our way of controlling the unknown. It
gives us a false sense of mastery. We label a person
— "intelligent," "lazy," "kind," "dangerous" — and
assume we know them. We label emotions, objects,
phenomena, even divinity itself. "This is God," we
say, pointing to an idol or a scripture. But how can
the infinite be captured in a word?

When we label, we are not engaging with reality —
we are engaging with our *idea* of reality. A child
sees a tree and marvels. An adult sees a tree and
moves on — because the word "tree" has replaced
the wonder.

A Real-Life Analogy: The Music Box

Imagine someone who has never heard music. You
give them a music box, and they open it. They see

gears, wires, and mechanisms. You explain how the box works — how the spring unwinds, how it turns the cylinder, how the pins pluck the comb to create sound. You label every part. The person nods and says, "Ah, I understand."

But the music itself — the feeling, the emotion, the silent beauty in the air — has not even been addressed.

This is our condition. We are dissecting the mechanism of life, but missing the music. We are describing trees, people, stars, and consciousness — but are we truly *experiencing* them?

Surface-Level Thinking: Because We Live on the Surface

Why is our understanding shallow? Because *we* are shallow in our perception. We think from the surface because we live on the surface. Our attention is external. We rarely look within. The journey inward — to the essence of life — is the only place where true knowing begins.

Knowing the uses of a tree is useful for survival. But knowing the *mystery* of the tree is essential for realization. The tree is not just an object — it is a living being. It belongs to a vast, interconnected dance of life — and it exists without our labels, without our approval, without our understanding.

It simply *is*.

And to encounter that "is-ness" without labelling — that is the beginning of wisdom.

The Humility of Not Knowing

Our understanding is not false — it is just incomplete. We must recognize the limit of our knowledge and the vastness of what lies beyond it. Labelling helps us organize, describe, and interact with the world. But it also conceals the deeper truth by replacing mystery with description.

To truly know something — whether a tree, a person, or life itself — we must go beyond the surface, beyond the names, beyond even thought. We must meet existence in silence.
And in that silence, perhaps, we may begin to *understand*.

The Language of the Soul: Beyond Words, Beyond Logic

There comes a moment in a human being's journey when all definitions collapse — not out of ignorance, but because one has touched the **core** of existence. This moment doesn't arise from reading a thousand books or perfecting logic, but from dissolving into life itself. A person who has *entered* their own being, who has journeyed to the heart of their own existence, no longer sees the world as separate or objective. Their description of life changes — or more accurately, it becomes unnecessary.

Their vision doesn't come from the intellect anymore.
It flows from **Bhava** — from feeling, from soul, from love.

Such a person may stand before a tree and say nothing.
Because what is there to say? Words belong to the surface.
But the tree — the tree speaks in silence.

The Tree as a Lover, Not an Object

To the ordinary mind, the tree is a resource. It is firewood, shade, oxygen, timber, or a thing of botanical interest. To the philosopher, it is a system of carbon and chlorophyll. To the scientist, it is a node in the ecosystem. To the religious, it might even be sacred.
But to one who has touched life deeply — the tree

is not any of these.
It is **alive**, it is **conscious**, and in some mysterious
way, it is **in love**.

Yes — the tree can fall in love. But not in the
human, possessive way. The tree's love is silent,
giving, unconditional. It stands there — through
wind, rain, drought, and time — offering shade,
fruit, fragrance, and beauty, asking for nothing in
return. If that is not love, what is?

The lover of life sees this. Not with the eyes, but
with the soul.
And the tree, in return, **speaks** — not through
words, but through presence.

You Cannot Understand the Soul Through the Mind

The problem is this: we are trying to understand life
using a language it doesn't speak.

Our minds are trained to dissect, to analyze, to
label. But the soul does not speak in categories. It
speaks in *feelings*. It does not measure, it melts. It
does not analyze, it surrenders.

So when we look at the tree with the mind, we
write essays. But when we look at it with the soul,
we cry. We sit beneath its shade and feel a stillness

we cannot explain. A breeze moves through its leaves, and something inside us also moves. There is no theory — only a deep sense of **belonging**.

The Tree Talks Back

Yes, the tree talks back — but only if you ask it correctly.
Not through logic, not through instruments — but through silence, reverence, and love.

You place your hand on its bark, close your eyes, and suddenly, you feel it — a pulse, a rhythm, a presence.
You don't know whether it's the tree or you — because now, the two are not separate.

You realize:
You never *knew* the tree.
You only *used* the tree.

And what we use, we never love.
What we love, we never destroy.

The Tragedy of Disconnection

We say trees have no feelings — but we never stopped to listen.
We ask, "Why should we care if the tree feels love or not?"

But we ask this only while we cut it down or burn it for heat.
At that moment, love is inconvenient. So we deny it.

But think — if trees had no feeling, why do we feel peace under their shade?
Why do we feel pain when we see a forest reduced to ash?
Why do we hug a tree when we grieve, and why does it comfort us without a word?

Because the soul knows.

Creation is the Work of Nature, Encroachment is the Work of Science, and Love is the Nature of the Soul

Science has its place. It helps us build, protect, predict, and improve.
But it cannot **create life** — it can only manipulate what life has already given.
It is **nature** that creates, silently, patiently, abundantly.

And it is **love** that sees creation for what it is: sacred, whole, alive.

The mind wants to use. The soul wants to unite.

Until we awaken the soul within us — the silent eye of love — we will continue to destroy what we do not understand.
But once love is awakened, once a person begins to feel the presence within all things, even a single leaf can become a scripture.

Return to the Sacred Vision

The one who has reached the core of his own being will never see a tree as "just a tree" again.
He may not say a word about it. He may not need to.
Because in that presence, he feels life — not explained, but *known*.
Not labeled, but *loved*.

Let us move beyond the language of logic and return to the language of love.
Let us feel again.
Because only then will the tree talk back.
Only then will life open her secrets to us.
Only then will we begin to live — not on the surface, but from the soul.

Vismayata: The Astonishment of Being

There are those rare ones who do not merely know about existence — they *know* existence itself.

These are the souls who, beyond appearances, grasp the living core of what *is*. For the rest of us, the path may begin with something as simple, yet profound, as falling in love with a tree.

When you truly fall in love with a tree, something subtle shifts within. You do not seek from it, you do not ask it to perform or provide. You care for it, not because it is useful, but because it *is*. This kind of love reveals the depth of your own being. For many, emotion remains only on the surface, like ripples on still water — momentary, beautiful, but lacking depth. Surface-level love is about taking. But when you have known the core — not only of a tree but of yourself, and of existence itself — love becomes eternal. And it flows from both sides.

This is the moment of *vismayata* — a sacred astonishment. It is not intellectual, not a discovery of science or analysis. It is a pure encounter. To try to understand it is to lose it, for love fades when dissected, and astonishment dies when reduced to theory.

So, do not try. Just sit beside a waterfall. Quietly. Listen. Not with the intent to study, but with the openness to *receive*. Let the sound of falling water become the rhythm of your own heart. Let it form a trance, not of forgetfulness, but of deep remembrance — of being, of presence. As you listen to the cascading waters, hear also the birds, the wind, the silence behind the sounds. That is where you begin to dissolve, softly, into yourself.

In that state, you realize something profound: suffering is not in the world — it is within. The external world is simply *what it is*. The filter is within you. If you look through the eyes of science, you will find structure, cause, and effect. If you look through the eyes of a poet, you will find metaphor, meaning, and beauty. If you look through the eyes of a singer, the world becomes melody. And if you look through the eyes of a lover, then everywhere, in everything — you will find love.

The world reflects back what you bring to it. This is not a trick of perception, but the deepest truth of reality. It is neither subjective nor objective, but relational — a dance between seer and seen, heart and world, silence and song.

To live in *vismayata* is to live in the sacred presence of life itself — not explained, but experienced. Not held in the hand, but held in the heart.

The Gaze of the Seer: Seeing the World Through Bhav

In the *Bhagavad Gita*, Krishna reveals a truth that is often missed in intellectual discourse, yet understood instantly by those who have tasted the mystery of life. He says, *"As you approach me, so I appear to you."* This is not merely a theological statement — it is a mirror to the nature of existence itself. The world is not as it is, but as *you are*.

Your gaze, your *bhav* — the emotional flavor or inner state from which you look at life — determines how life responds. If your heart is angry, then the world seems full of reasons to be enraged. If your heart is burdened with fear, then every shadow becomes a threat. But if love lives within you, then even in a storm, you will find beauty. This is not idealism; it is the subtle alchemy of perception.

The world does not offer only one face. It presents countless forms and flavors. That is why it is entirely possible for you to love something that another person despises. It is possible for a song to bring tears of joy to you while it irritates someone else. There is no objective right or wrong here — only perspectives, only mirrors. We each hold a lens, polished or foggy, joyful or broken, through which we see the play of reality. Thus, the world is not fixed, it is reflected.

Those who radiate anger, hatred, or bitterness are not showing the world as it is — they are revealing themselves. They deserve compassion, not condemnation, because such expressions are signs of inner suffering. It is the hurting who often hurt others. Just as a lamp cannot throw light without being lit within, love cannot shine unless it is already burning in your heart.

This deep insight is embodied in the figure of Krishna, the most paradoxical and mysterious of all divine avatars in Hindu thought. Krishna does not fit into any tidy definition of godhood. He breaks the mold. He has 16,000 queens, he steals butter and clothes in his youth, he plays tricks, and yet he delivers the most sublime teachings of the *Gita*. He protects the dignity of Draupadi in the Kaurava court, enters the war of *Mahabharata* without wielding a weapon, and dances with abandon with the *Gopis*. He is a god who laughs, who weeps, who fights, who flees. He is a warrior and a trickster, a lover and a mystic.

No religion or dogma can fully contain such a being. He is not a god shaped by morality — he is a mirror of existence itself. That is why even saints revere him, not for his actions but for his essence. They look beyond the stories, beyond the surface, to the truth he reveals — the truth of *dharma*, of *karma*, of cosmic play (*leela*). Saints know where to focus: not on the form, but on the formless truth that shines through it.

Every avatar, every prophet, every realized being — whether it is Krishna, Buddha, Jesus, or anyone else — is pointing toward the same truth. But the expressions are many, the forms are many, the metaphors are many. Truth itself is one, or perhaps it is better to say — truth is *zero*. It is *nothing*, in the deepest and most liberating sense. It cannot be named, because naming is labeling, and labeling limits. The moment you define the truth, you bind it to your words — and in doing so, you miss it.

Truth cannot be held in language. It can only be known in silence — in the language of the soul.

So do not be quick to label. Ask instead: *what is the one that shines behind all forms?* The Gita, the Bible, the Dhammapada, the Tao Te Ching — they are not the truth, but they point toward it. They are fingers pointing to the moon. If you get caught in the finger, you miss the moon.

In this light, Krishna is not just a figure from myth or scripture. He becomes a mirror, a symbol of the vastness of being, the multidimensionality of truth. Whether saint or sinner, warrior or beggar, all can find something of themselves in him. For he is not asking you to be like him — he is showing you how to see beyond labels, into the heart of reality.

And when you begin to see that way — with the eyes of *bhav*, with the language of the soul — the world no longer appears divided. It becomes one. Then there is no "other." There is only astonishment. *Vismayata*.

The Politics of Divinity: When Truth Becomes Inconvenient

Imagine, for a moment, that both Jesus and Muhammad had taken birth in India. According to traditional Hindu beliefs, this would mean the cycle of divine avatars would be nearly complete. Ten avatars — *Dashavatara* — fulfilled. And then, just one vacant slot would remain. The "Kalki" avatar. That final messianic figure, the cosmic liberator, the one who arrives at the end of *Kali Yuga* to restore *dharma* and destroy *adharma*. But what if the world — or those who claim to guard the truth — are not ready to accept that completion?

The number of avatars, then, becomes more than symbolic. It becomes political. If the list is full, there is no room for new revelations, no space for new awakenings. There is a silent consensus that says: "Let's not acknowledge anyone else now — unless, of course, it's convenient." There must always be room for a *trump card*, a last-minute savior to be used if the structures of control begin to collapse. Like the proverbial **Mandari Ka Bandar** — the trained monkey used in street performances — a spectacle to regain attention and obedience.

What, then, becomes the qualification for the modern-day avatar?

Miracles no longer impress. Science has peeled back the layers of mystery. The splitting of the atom, the mapping of the genome, and the distant echoes of the Big Bang have replaced fireballs and levitations. In today's world, an avatar must be more than divine — he must be *human*, deeply so. A mystic with the insight of a saint, the strategy of a politician, and the subtlety of a diplomat. He must navigate the world's complexity without being torn apart by it.

Because truth, in its raw form, is no longer welcomed.

The age of those who speak directly — like Buddha or Osho — seems to be over. We forget that Buddha was stoned and banished. That Osho was exiled and ridiculed. And why? Not because they were wrong — but because they were *right*. They disturbed the status quo. They exposed the hypocrisies that had built entire empires of belief. And those who profit from these empires — religious, political, or cultural — will never tolerate someone who threatens to shut down their shops of illusion.

The avatar, then, is only accepted under one condition: *he must play by the rules we create for him.*

He must be born in a land deemed sacred. He must align with a religion deemed valid. He must support the structures of power, or at least not question them too loudly. Whatever truths he reveals, whatever wisdom he shares — none of it will matter if he doesn't fit the image already carved in stone. And if he dares to step outside that frame?

We will disown him. Or worse, we will kill him —
and then build a temple in his name.

That is the history of truth. First, we reject it. Then
we distort it. And finally, when it's safe and no
longer dangerous, we sanctify it.

If a Jesus were to return today, unfiltered and
unbranded, he would be crucified again — not by
Romans, but by the very people who claim to
follow him. If a Buddha were to walk barefoot
through modern India, speaking uncomfortable
truths, he would be dismissed as mad or dangerous.
Not because their truths have lost value — but
because our *attachment to illusion* has only grown
stronger.

This is the paradox of divinity: the more true it is,
the less welcome it becomes. And yet, in the
silence beyond systems and dogmas, the real
seeker knows — truth does not require approval.
The avatar is not chosen by society; he is born of
the *need* of the time. Whether we acknowledge
him or not, he comes. Whether we stone him or
worship him, he speaks. And whether we
manipulate his words or preserve them, he sows
the seed.

Not for the crowd. But for the one who listens.

Truth, the Lost Child in the Crowd

Truth — the God — does not operate by the rules we have created. It does not discriminate. It does not favor one culture, one religion, one name over another. Truth is like light: it falls on all equally, but we see it only through the windows we have built. Sometimes, it shines through Krishna. Sometimes through Jesus. Sometimes through Buddha. These are not rivals; they are different languages spoken by the same silence.

Each of them knew the truth — or perhaps it is better to say, they became the truth in their own way. Krishna saw the truth and understood the mind of the world. So, he walked the path of diplomacy, blending wisdom with the practicalities of politics. He danced and deceived, loved and strategized, not because he was confused — but because he was complete. He was the balance between play and power, between spirit and society.

Buddha also saw the truth. But his path was unique — quiet, clean, and inward. He renounced the palace, the kingdom, and the world itself to sit under a tree. He became a doctor of the soul, diagnosing the disease of suffering and offering the Eightfold Path as a method of healing. He spoke of *dukkha*, of craving, and the possibility of liberation not through dogma but awareness. A mystic, a scientist, a philosopher, and a psychologist — Buddha combined them all into one breath of clarity.

And yet, despite the beauty of their teachings, humanity has a habit of rejecting those who speak directly. Socrates, who asked uncomfortable questions, was forced to drink poison. Jesus, who spoke of love beyond boundaries, was crucified. Buddha, despite his non-violence, was banished from places. Osho, who exposed hypocrisies, was exiled. The pattern is clear: when someone speaks naked truth — without fear, without the comfort of tradition — society defends itself, sometimes violently.

A modern echo of this can be seen in **Julian Assange**, who revealed uncomfortable truths about power and war, and has faced relentless persecution since. He did not perform miracles; he revealed documents. But even that truth — factual, unfiltered — was too much. The truth shakes the foundations of institutions built on control. It threatens the "shops" of religion, politics, and commerce. If truth enters, hypocrisy must leave — and no one wants to close their shop.

What most fail to see is that God — or truth — is not bound to form. It presents itself not only in the enlightened, but also in trees, silence, laughter, loss, and love. It is not exclusive. The problem lies in our addiction to labels. We say "God," "truth," "enlightenment" — but these are just fingers pointing. Worshipping the finger misses the view. Every name we give becomes a wall, when the truth is meant to be a sky.

Realization is the only way. Not belief, not ritual, not blind tradition. When you *see* with your own eyes, not through borrowed thoughts, the fog begins to lift. Truth is not far. It is here, now, waiting for a silent space within you to echo back its voice.

Take **Ravidas**, the 15th-century Indian mystic from a lower caste. His poetry was drenched in universal truth, defying the caste structure. He was rejected by society, yet his words survived. Even today, many try to claim him, to wrap him in religious identity, but what he spoke transcended religion. The new is always buried under the old, the original voice drowned in the noise of echoes. The system will always try to say, "This was already there." It's a defense mechanism — a way to tame the wildness of revelation.

This is the tragedy of our age: religion and politics have merged. Politics is now the new religion. Religion has become political. One controls bodies, the other controls minds. Both are terrified of a free soul, a voice that cannot be owned.

So where is truth in all this?

It is like a small child lost in the crowd — innocent, fragile, calling out, but drowned in the noise of slogans, rituals, and ideologies. The child does not shout. It waits for someone to notice. And most people are too busy looking up at the sky to see the truth already holding their hand.

But there is hope.

As long as one person listens. As long as one heart turns inward. As long as even one being dares to live without lies, the child is not lost. That one person becomes the seed, and from that seed, forests can grow.

So yes, truth is a child — but it is a child of fire. Lost, but luminous. Misunderstood, but eternal.

Love is the Path Toward God
— A Journey from the Heart to the Infinite

In the end, all paths dissolve. All philosophies collapse. All questions fall silent. What remains is love.

It may seem like a simple word—just four letters. But behind it is the doorway to the divine. Love is not just an emotion. It is not a romantic fantasy, nor merely affection for another person. Love is a force. A fire. A light that dissolves the boundary between you and the other. It is the only real bridge between the soul and the source. Love, in its purest form, is the path toward God.

God is not a person sitting on a throne above the clouds. God is not a judge or ruler. God is the ultimate mystery—unseen, unheard, untouched. So how do we approach something we cannot see? Not with logic. Not with rituals. But with the heart.

Love is the only language that God understands.

The mystics of every tradition have known this. Meera, Rumi, Kabir, Francis of Assisi, Rabia Basri, Jesus, and even Krishna himself—all spoke the language of love. Not dry commandments, but ecstatic surrender. Not fear of punishment, but intoxication with the divine presence.

Rumi danced in circles, drunk on the wine of divine love. He wrote, *"I have seen the Beloved in every face, in every leaf, in every breath."* His words were not poetry—they were fire. They came from an inner explosion of love that destroyed the boundaries between lover and beloved.

Meera, the Rajput princess who abandoned her kingdom, sang day and night for her beloved Krishna. She didn't care about society's judgments, family restrictions, or religious rules. Her love burned away everything else. She said, *"I have found my God, and I will not let him go."*

Even **Jesus**, when asked what the greatest commandment is, said nothing about laws or fear. He said, *"Love the Lord your God with all your heart, and love your neighbor as yourself."* That was it. Love for God. Love for each other. Everything else is detail.

Because love has a strange power—it dissolves the ego.

In love, you forget yourself. You become fluid, open, vulnerable. You step out of the armor of the mind and stand naked before existence. And in that nakedness, something beautiful happens—you are no longer separate. That illusion of "I" and "you" disappears. And when separation disappears, God appears.

Modern life, however, has turned love into a commodity. Swipe left, swipe right. Conditional love. Strategic affection. We say "I love you" but often mean "I need you." Real love is not about possession. It is not about fulfilling personal emptiness. Real love is the overflowing of being—it gives, not because it lacks, but because it is full.

Love is like a candle. It burns itself to give light to others. It dies in the process, but in its death, it reveals beauty.

To walk the path of love is not easy. It is not soft and sweet as people imagine. It is fierce. It is dangerous. Because to truly love means to risk everything—to be broken, to be rejected, to be vulnerable, to dissolve. And yet, the reward is the greatest gift life has to offer: union.

Think of **Radha and Krishna**. Their love was not just between two people. It was symbolic—the longing of the soul (Radha) for the eternal (Krishna). Their dance, the *Raas Leela*, was not a physical event—it was a cosmic metaphor. A union of the finite with the infinite.

In the Sufi tradition, **Rabia Basri** once said, "O God, if I worship You for fear of hell, burn me in hell. If I worship You for desire of heaven, exclude me from heaven. But if I worship You for You alone, do not deny me Your eternal beauty." That is love. Pure. Without demand.

Even in the East, **Bhakti Yoga**—the path of devotion—teaches that God is not something to be known intellectually, but something to be loved wholeheartedly. The bhakta does not argue; he dances. He does not analyze; he surrenders.

This is not weakness. This is the highest courage.

In a world full of noise, love is silence.
In a world full of walls, love is a bridge.
In a world full of masks, love is truth.

To love is to return home—not to a physical place, but to your original nature. That's why children are so radiant. They haven't yet learned how to hide their love. Look into the eyes of a child or a saint, and you'll see the same light. Pure presence. That is what we've lost, and that is what love brings back.

Love is not about finding God somewhere else. It is about realizing that you were never separate in the first place. That the very source of your heartbeat, your breath, your being—is divine. When you love deeply, selflessly, unconditionally—you don't reach God. You remember you are already in God.

You are a wave in the ocean of the divine.
Love is the moment you stop pretending to be separate.

So yes—there are many paths. The path of knowledge, the path of meditation, the path of discipline. But all of them, if they are real, must pass through the valley of love. Without love, spirituality is dry. Like a river with no water. Like a temple with no deity. Like a body with no soul.

Let your life be soaked in love—not just for a person, but for the very miracle of being alive. Love the trees, the sky, the silence, the stranger. Love yourself. And in that love, you will begin to see glimpses of the eternal.

Because love is not the destination.

Love is the path. Love is the guide. Love is God.

Slavery: The Deepest Wound in the History of Humanlty
A Reflection on Cruelty, Injustice, and the Legacy of Human Hatred

Slavery is not just a crime—it is one of the darkest, most brutal sins ever committed by humanity. A stain so deep that even centuries later, its shadows continue to haunt our collective soul. To enslave another human being—to strip them of freedom, dignity, and identity—is to kill their spirit while keeping their body alive. It is a slow-motion murder of the human essence.

Throughout history, during wars and invasions, villages were burned to the ground, cities reduced to ash, and those who survived the massacre were not spared—they were enslaved. The old were killed, and the young—especially women and children—were captured, shackled, and sold like cattle. Their homes were looted, their families torn apart, their futures sold to the highest bidder. Brothers sent to different cities, mothers separated from their babies, lovers lost forever—destinies shattered like broken glass under the feet of conquerors.

These human beings were treated not as people, but as property. Stripped of names, given numbers. Their voices erased. Their rights denied. The owners could command anything, and the slaves had no choice but to obey. To resist was to be punished. To flee was to be hunted. To disobey was to be tortured, humiliated, or killed—with no law to protect them, no justice to be found.

Can you imagine such a life?

Imagine being unable to leave a room without permission. Imagine being told when to eat, sleep, speak, or even urinate. Imagine your body being used, abused, and discarded as entertainment. Imagine being forced to fight another human being—another slave—just to amuse your master and his guests. And if you lose, you die. If you win, you suffer longer.

Women, in particular, bore the worst of this cruelty. Exploited not only as laborers but as objects of lust. Raped repeatedly, forced to give birth to children they could not raise—children born not out of love but violence. These babies too would be sold or killed, continuing the nightmare like a cursed cycle.

Some slaves broke. Some surrendered. Some took their own lives just to escape the unending torture.

For many, death was not the enemy—it was freedom. The only peace they could imagine. A quiet release from the unbearable noise of suffering.

The Voice of the Survivors

The horrors of slavery are not just distant shadows—they are carved into the memories of those who endured it. Here are fragments of their stories, echoes of their pain.

Olaudah Equiano, a Nigerian boy kidnapped at the age of 11, was sold into slavery and transported to the Americas. In his memoir, he recalls the moment he was separated from his sister: *"The shrieks of the women, and the groans of the dying, rendered the whole a scene of horror almost inconceivable."* He would later buy his freedom and become one of the earliest voices to expose the brutal reality of the transatlantic slave trade.

Harriet Jacobs, an African-American woman born into slavery, wrote in her autobiography *Incidents in the Life of a Slave Girl* about hiding in an attic crawlspace for seven years to escape the sexual abuse of her owner: *"Only by experiencing it could anyone know the depth of degradation and misery."* Her story exposed how enslaved women suffered doubly—as laborers and as targets of exploitation.

Frederick Douglass, once whipped so severely that he nearly died, wrote about the psychological destruction of slavery: *"I have often been so pinched with hunger, that I have fought with the dog... for the smallest bones thrown away."* He escaped slavery, learned to read in secret, and later became one of the most powerful orators for human dignity.

From India to Africa, from the Americas to the Middle East, slavery left scars on every continent.

In modern Mauritania, Moulkheir Mint Yarba, a woman born into hereditary slavery, described how her master raped her repeatedly and forced her to raise children born from that abuse—only to see them sold into slavery, too. *"They took my children away,"* she whispered. *"They never came back."*

Even now, countless modern slaves work in brick kilns, as domestic workers, in mines, in brothels. One escaped bonded laborer from Nepal, Kali, said, *"We were paid nothing. Beaten if we rested. My child died from a fever because they wouldn't let us go."*

These are not just stories. These are open wounds.

If we, as a species, were capable of such cruelty toward our fellow humans, how can we ever expect true compassion for the Earth? For the forests we cut down without regret? For the animals we cage and slaughter? For the rivers we poison, the air we darken? A species that once caged its own kind, sold them, raped them, broke them—how will it ever learn to live in harmony with nature?

We are still suffering from the disease of hatred and greed. We are not fully healed. The ghosts of slavery still whisper in the corners of our history. They cry out from the blood-soaked soil, from the ancient chains buried under time, from the stories that were never told because the victims were never allowed to speak.

We often talk about building a better future. But what kind of future can be built on the backs of such inhumanity? How can we expect peace if we've never made peace with our past? How can we talk of progress if we haven't faced the horror we once called normal?

There is no other creature on this planet that behaves the way we have. No animal enslaves its own kind. No bird sells another bird. No wolf chains another wolf. We are the only species that has turned against itself in such systematic, horrifying ways.

What happened during those centuries of slavery is not just a chapter in history—it is a mirror. A brutal reflection of what humans are capable of when love dies and power becomes god.

Yes, we have grown. Yes, slavery in its legal form has ended in many countries. But has the mentality ended? Has the greed, the dehumanization, the exploitation truly stopped? Or have we just changed the form? Modern slavery still exists—hidden in sweatshops, in human trafficking, in child labor, in abused domestic workers. The chains may look different now, but they still exist.

We must never forget. We must never erase or soften this truth.

Because to forget the pain of the past is to allow its seeds to grow again.

Slavery was not just a crime against individuals—it was a crime against humanity itself. It was a betrayal of our highest potential. A failure of empathy, of justice, of soul. And until we truly understand the depth of that pain, we will never be free.

Freedom is not just the absence of chains. It is the presence of dignity.

And until every human being can live with that dignity, we remain, in some way, enslaved to our own darkness.

Slavery Has Changed Its Face, But Not Disappeared
A Reflection on the Illusion of Freedom in Modern Society

Slavery in India was officially abolished in 1843 with the passage of the Indian Slavery Act. A law was signed, some chains were broken, and the practice of buying and selling humans was declared illegal. On paper, it was a victory. On the ground, the echoes of slavery still whisper.

But here's the real question: **Are we truly free today?**

Look around. Peel back the surface. Strip away the masks of progress and modernity, and you'll see: slavery still exists—it's just rebranded. The chains have become invisible. The prisons are now made of expectations, fear, competition, and debt. We no longer call it slavery, because now we don't even realize we're in it.

In ancient slavery, the slave knew he was not free. Today, we are conditioned not to notice. That's more dangerous. A cage you see can be escaped. But when the bars are invisible, you might live your entire life inside it without ever knowing.

The Birth of a Predefined Life

Every child today is born not into freedom, but into **a predefined script**—a machine-written manual on "how to exist" that society hands down without question. From the moment they open their eyes, the expectations begin: walk this path, speak this language, worship this god, score these marks, wear these clothes, get this job, marry by this age, never question.

We don't raise humans anymore—we manufacture them.

We crush their curiosity under the weight of rules. We label their wonder as distraction. We call their truth rebellious. A child born with dreams is taught quickly: dreams are dangerous. Better follow the system. Obey. Fit in. Don't think. Don't feel too much. Don't ask too many questions.

The greatest crime we've committed isn't war or pollution—it's the **killing of the soul** while the body still breathes.

The New Masters and Their Tools

Who are the new slave-owners?

They aren't kings or traders now. They are systems, corporations, media, ideologies. They are abstract but real, subtle but strong. They control us through **desire** and **fear**.

We are made to believe we need more to be happy. A better job. A bigger house. A shinier phone. A more attractive body. We spend our entire lives chasing things that never satisfy the soul. And in that chase, we become servants. Slaves. Programmed units following commands that were never ours to begin with.

The 9-to-5 grind. The toxic competition. The constant comparison. The pressure to succeed according to someone else's definition. The fear of being left behind. All of it: **a quiet slavery**—one we willingly accept.

Rebels Are Treated Like Threats

Sometimes—rarely—a human is born who doesn't accept the script. A Buddha. A Kabir. A Jesus. An Osho. These people **refuse to be programmed**. They ask the dangerous questions. They walk their own path. They burn the script. And what does society do to such people?

It condemns them. Kills them. Labels them as mad, heretic, threat.

Because **truth is dangerous in a world built on lies**.

The basic nature of a human being is not to obey blindly—it is to explore. The soul doesn't crave wealth or power. It craves **freedom**. It craves **truth**. But we have failed to offer either. We are still building systems that reward obedience and punish authenticity.

From Greed to Hatred, and Hatred to Collapse

Humanity, time and again, has chosen **greed over compassion**. That greed leads to division. Division leads to discrimination. Discrimination breeds hatred. Hatred gives birth to violence. And here we are, stuck in the loop for thousands of years.

In the name of better futures, we have sacrificed the present. We've looted nature. We've enslaved one another. We've silenced the poets, the prophets, the mystics—the very ones who tried to wake us up.

We have built societies where **to die feels easier than to live**.

Ask yourself: how many people around you are truly alive? Not just functioning, but alive in the heart, in the spirit? Very few. Most are sleepwalking—smiling outside, screaming inside. We are **a civilization of ghosts wearing suits**.

So What Now?

True abolition of slavery won't come from laws. It will come from **awakening**.

From every individual realizing they've been programmed—and choosing to break free. Choosing to unlearn. Choosing to reclaim their curiosity. Choosing to live from their own truth, not borrowed beliefs.

To be free is not to have choices made for you, but to make your own.
To be free is not to obey, but to understand.
To be free is not just to exist, but to **live**—fully, courageously, authentically.

We must become the rebels again.

Slavery, Discrimination, and the Madness of Modern Civilization
A Call to Wake Up and Become Truly Human

Even our divine religions teach us love, peace, and compassion. The prophets, the sages, the enlightened ones—they all spoke of one universal truth: **to love is to be free, to hurt is to fall into darkness.**

So why is the world like this?

Why is it that everyone craves love, yet what we receive is mostly hatred? Why does every soul long for freedom, yet live in silent chains? Why are the teachings of Krishna, Jesus, Buddha, and

Muhammad on every tongue—but rarely in practice?

It's madness. It's not civilization—it's a *well-decorated circus*.

The Modern Circus of Slavery

People often say slavery is over. The law changed. But look closely. The cage just became fancier. The hunter became a corporation. The whip turned into a paycheck. And the lion? It's us.

A lion belongs in the jungle, wild and proud. But in a circus, the lion is starved until it obeys. It forgets the jungle. It forgets the roar. All it remembers is the pain of punishment.

Just like us.

Middle-class families work 12 to 15 hours a day for a salary that barely covers their living. Year after year, the same routine. The same grind. Dreams are buried beneath bills. Creativity dies under deadlines. And worst of all, **most people never even ask "why?"**

This is the quiet slavery of the modern age. Not of chains—but of **invisible pressure**. Not of whips—

but of **fear of failure**. Not of masters—but of **systems we didn't choose** but silently follow.

Greed Has Replaced God

We are the most intelligent species on this planet—so where is the responsibility that should come with that intelligence?

Instead of protecting life, we exploit it. We destroy forests for buildings, pollute rivers for factories, and poison the air we breathe. The same people who can't plant a tree on Earth are dreaming of starting colonies on Mars.

What insanity is this?

How can you save a new world when you've failed to respect the one you have?

The future we are building is terrifying: polluted air, low oxygen levels, overpopulation, dying species, disappearing water. And yet—we still don't stop. We want more. Always more. Greed blinds us. And greed has a loud, ugly twin: **discrimination**.

Discrimination: The Second Great Crime of Humanity

Discrimination is pain dressed as power.

It is a wound in the soul of humanity—infected, untreated, and bleeding for centuries. Race, religion, caste, gender, nationality, language—human beings have found infinite ways to divide themselves. And in every division, someone rises, someone falls. Someone rules, someone suffers.

Thousands of wars have been fought to prove superiority. Millions have died for flags and gods and borders. And for what? A few lines in history books. A few monuments. A few graves.

We have misunderstood everything—even God.

We began discriminating in His name. Instead of seeing the divine in every being, we started drawing lines: "my God vs your God", "my heaven vs your hell".

What madness. Even **Gods must weep** when they see what we've done in their name.

Wake Up, or Die Slowly

Imagine doing nothing for a month. Just observe. Become like a silent watch—no action, no reaction. See the world as it is. If you can see deeply, without illusion, you'll realize this system is broken at the root.

And if your response is, "Well, we can't do anything, the world is like this,"
then I say—you're **not worthy of being called a human being.**

Because the true human being is not a machine.
Not a puppet.
Not a silent observer.

The true human is a seeker. A creator. A rebel. A lover. A protector of life.

From Slavery to Freedom, From Hatred to Love

Slavery and discrimination are not just crimes. They are **curses**—and we are still living under their spell. They are born from **greed and hatred**. And until we awaken, they will not die.

The only thing that can break this spell is **love**. Not romantic love. Not weak love. But the **fiery, fearless love** that Muhammad felt when he bought slaves just to set them free. That Buddha radiated when he left his kingdom to end suffering. That Jesus embodied when he forgave even those who crucified him.

These were not weak men. These were warriors of the soul. And they all walked one path—the path of **love**.

But don't misunderstand love.

Love is not passive. It is the most **active force in the universe**. Love doesn't just accept reality—it transforms it. Love doesn't tolerate injustice—it ends it. Love is not blind—it sees everything and still chooses compassion.

Our Mission: From Human to Universal Being

We were not born to be slaves. We were born to be awake.

Our mission must not be just to survive, but to **become human** in the truest sense. And then to go beyond even that—to become a **universal being**: free from greed, free from hatred, full of awareness and love.

The choice is in our hands.
Either live like lions in the jungle, proud and free.
Or like lions in the circus—trained, hungry, and
confused.

The time to wake up is **now**.

The Poem of God: Understanding the Divine Through the Universe

This world, this universe—it is not just an accident, not just a random scattering of atoms and galaxies. It is a *poem*, written in silence, shaped in eternity. And the poet? That is God. Not a man in the sky. Not a figure with a crown. But a *presence*, an *artist*, a *mystery* so deep that even silence fails to describe him.

If you want to know a poet, you don't interrogate him—you read his work. You don't ask him to explain—you dive into his verses, you sit with his silences. You let the rhythm touch you. You feel the pain between the lines, the joy behind the metaphors.

To understand God, look at his creation. That's

where he speaks. That's where he hides. That's where he reveals.

But we don't listen.
We keep shouting, "Where is God? Why doesn't he speak?"
He *is* speaking. Through the stars, the trees, the rain, the laughter of a child, the cry of an old man, the wind that passes through without asking permission. But to hear him—you must learn his language.

And his language is not made of words.
It's made of *silence*.
It's made of *stillness*.
It's made of *presence*.
And above all—it's made of *love*.

What We Call Love is Not Love

But what we call "love" today is not that language.
It is not divine.
It is not free.
It is not unconditional.

It's just a polished version of violence.

We say, "I love you," but what we mean is, "I want you."
We say, "I care for you," but what we do is control, possess, limit.
We try to bind the one we love. We put them in golden cages. We expect them to behave the way we want. That is not love—that is **ego wearing perfume**.

True love is not bondage—it is freedom.
True love is not clinging—it is letting go.
True love is not needing—it is overflowing.

Look at God. He created us, yet never interferes. He gave us life, and then stepped back—gave us choice, pain, joy, mistakes, discovery. He could have programmed us like machines. But he didn't. Why?

Because love doesn't control. Love trusts. Love lets you fall so you can learn to rise.
This is divine parenting. This is real love. But we have forgotten it.

Pleasure in Violence: The Human Tragedy

We, as humans, have made violence our essence.
Not just in wars, but in love, in ambition, in religion,

in daily interactions. We dominate. We compete.
We exploit. And we call it life.

Why?

Because violence gives a false sense of power.
Control gives a false sense of security.
And in our emptiness, we cling to these illusions.

But this is not living. This is **surviving through manipulation**.
And it's the root of all misery.

Where there is bondage, there can be no love.
Where there is fear, there can be no God.
Where there is desire to possess, the soul is absent.

Returning to the Divine Language

To hear God, we must unlearn everything.
We must let go of our versions of love, power, success.
We must sit with trees, with rivers, with ourselves.

We must stop trying to conquer love—and instead,
become love.

Because love, in its highest form, is not a
relationship. It's a *state of being*.

It is *not between two people*, but between the soul and the whole existence.

So What Must We Do?

We must stop pretending to know love.
We must stop claiming to own others.
We must stop asking God to show up—and start seeing that he never left.

And most of all,
we must learn to love **like God loves**—
without expectations, without conditions, without fear.

When you love like that,
you don't just understand the poet.
You become the poem.

This is my fourth Sutra Love is the only way to find truth.

Love and Light: Two Currents of the Same River

Love and light are parallel. If love turns inward, it becomes light. If light shines outward, it becomes love. These are not opposites; they are the same essence flowing in different directions. Light means you have forgotten yourself completely. It happens when you lose yourself in something so entirely—in a sunset, a moment of silence, a wordless connection—that only the moment remains. That immersion, that deep presence, is light. And when that inner clarity reaches out, touches another, opens into the world—it is love.

But love, as we commonly understand it, is not what this is. What most people call love is often attachment, need, or fear wrapped in sweetness. True love is not something you can trap, define, or hold onto. It is like the wind—a powerful wave that comes, tickles you, fills you with fragrance, and moves on. You don't chase the wind; you feel it, smile, and let it go. If you run after it, trying to hold that one moment, you get lost, trapped. Because no one can stop the wind. No one can possess love.

Love is not attachment. It is, in fact, detachment. It arises in freedom and gives freedom. It is not a chain, it is a door opening into the vast. To confuse it with bonding is to misunderstand it completely.

So when I say there is no God in the temple, I am not denying people's faith. I cannot question their faith, because **"Shraddha"** is a beautiful feeling. It means surrender. It means offering yourself without hesitation. And surrender, in its pure form, is a path in itself. A person who surrenders completely dissolves—and that dissolving is the key to love. In love, too, you lose yourself. People looking from the outside might call it madness. But madness and love are not the same, even if they appear similar.

In love, you open up from within and become free. In madness, you get trapped both inside and out. In madness, all doors close. In love, there are no walls, no locks, no limits. Love makes everything beautiful. It changes your eyes, your breath, your being. Even the most ordinary things start to glow. Madness shrinks you. Love makes you vast.

Imagine a seed. Madness is the fear that wraps itself around the seed and never lets it grow. Love is that middle tree, grown tall and alive, on which a flower has blossomed. Fear exists in madness. In love, fear cannot survive.

And here is the truth: the language of madness can only be understood by the mad. But the language of love? That is the language of the universe. The trees speak it. The sky echoes it. The stars whisper it.

Try defining love, and you will get lost. Try putting it in a frame, and it will escape. Love cannot be

taught. It cannot be grasped. It must be felt. That's
why saints, poets, and mystics often confuse us.
Because they try to describe the indescribable.

Take Meera Bai, for example. She had understood
love. People called her mad, but she was not. She
had reached that ultimate surrender, that devotion
which looks like madness to the ordinary world.
She left behind her palace, her status, her wealth—
not out of duty, but out of love. Love for Krishna,
who did not even have a body. Her love was not for
a man, it was for a presence, a fragrance, a
remembrance of the divine.

But what gave rise to that devotion? It was her
Guru, Raidas Ji. He planted the seed of love
inwardly, and it bloomed outwardly as Meera's love
for Krishna. That is the difference between
madness and devotion. Meera was not lost. She
had found herself.

Devotion is love directed outward with focus
inward. And love is devotion turned into presence.
They are two sides of one truth.

And here lies a subtle but beautiful distinction:
women often find meditation through love. They
begin with feeling and descend into stillness. Men,
on the other hand, often find love through

meditation. They begin with silence and rise into emotion. Eventually, both meet in the heart—in that space where love and light become one.

And that is where God waits. Not in temples. Not in scriptures. But in the heart where love blossoms without bondage. In the light that burns without shadow.

That is the real shrine.

<u>**Sutra - 5**</u>

Dharmikta: The Subtle Art of Conscious Living

In a world shaped by religious traditions, cultural values, and philosophical systems, the word *Dharma* carries immense weight. We are all familiar with the many types of Dharma—be it individual, societal, professional, or spiritual. Each one offers guidance, a kind of compass to navigate life. But beyond all these, there exists a more refined and personal dimension of being: *Dharmikta.*

Dharmikta is not a code one memorizes or a doctrine one must follow. It is the natural fragrance of conscious living. While *Dharma* is often external—rules, roles, and responsibilities— *Dharmikta* is internal. It arises not from obligation but from awareness. It is not about being religious in a formal sense; it is about being sensitive to life, moment by moment. One does not need to follow any particular Dharma to become *Dharmik.* A little consciousness in daily life is enough.

Consider the simple act of eating. We eat every day, yet rarely do we do it consciously. The food we consume provides nourishment to the body. When chosen wisely—with the right nutrients and in the right quantity—it becomes medicine. But when consumed mindlessly, even the healthiest food can cause suffering. Overeating is one such example. When we eat more than the body needs, our system has to divert a large portion of energy toward digestion. This makes us feel heavy, lazy, and often sleepy right after meals. The body's energy, instead of being available for creativity, movement, or awareness, is tied up in processing excess food.

Let's take a real-life example. Imagine a working professional, Ravi, who eats a large lunch every day at the office. Initially, it's a comforting routine—a full plate, a brief escape from work stress. But soon he notices a pattern: after lunch, his focus drops, he becomes irritable, and he feels the need for an afternoon nap or coffee to stay awake. His productivity declines, and he begins to suffer from mild digestive issues.

Eventually, Ravi visits a holistic health consultant. The advice is simple yet profound: eat smaller meals, but eat four times a day instead of three. Balance your intake. Listen to your body. Ravi follows this advice. Slowly, his energy returns. He remains alert throughout the day, his mood improves, and his digestion stabilizes. What changed? Not just the food—but the consciousness with which he engaged in eating.

This is *Dharmikta*. It is not just about what you eat, but how you eat. It is about being present with your body, listening to its rhythm, and respecting its intelligence.

The body and mind are intimately connected. If there is imbalance in the body—due to overeating, lack of movement, or poor sleep—it affects the mind directly. Similarly, if the mind is full of restless or negative thoughts, the body responds with fatigue, tension, or illness. These are not separate systems. The energy of thought becomes physical sensation. The energy of physical activity shapes the clarity of thought.

Therefore, to be *Dharmik* in the true sense is to be aware of this deep connection. It is to respect the intelligence of both body and mind. It is to recognize that health is not merely the absence of disease, but the presence of harmony. When energy flows evenly throughout the system, when neither the body nor the mind is overloaded or neglected, life becomes effortless. Peace arises not from control, but from balance.

Dharmikta is not confined to temples or scriptures. It lives in the kitchen, in the breath, in how we speak to others, in how we treat our own body. Every moment gives us the opportunity to live consciously. And when we do, we do not merely follow Dharma—we embody it.

The Alchemy of Thought and Energy: Understanding "Vikshipta"

There is a subtle yet undeniable connection between our thoughts and our physical body. Every emotion we feel, every reaction we experience, is not just psychological—it is physiological. The body doesn't merely *host* the mind; it *responds* to it. This truth is so immediate and observable that it needs no philosophy to validate it—only awareness.

Take the simple example of alcohol. Most people know its effect—it alters your state of consciousness, slows your responses, and interferes with brain function. What many don't realize is that alcohol directly affects the brain's cellular activity. Many neurons are damaged or numbed temporarily. That's why even a small amount can make someone feel light-headed or uninhibited. The same physical impact is mirrored in our emotional experiences, even without consuming a substance.

Let's shift our focus to thought—something invisible, internal, yet powerful. Imagine for a moment that a man sees a beautiful woman, or is exposed to sexually stimulating content. Almost instantly, he feels a response in his body: perhaps a racing heart, a stirring in his core, a rush of heat. What happened? There was no physical contact— just a thought, a visual input, and yet the body reacts as though something real has occurred. This is because thought is not just a mental event; it is energetic. It triggers biochemical and physiological changes in the body.

This is the nature of *Kriya*—action—and *Pratikriya*—reaction. The body responds immediately to the energetic signature of a thought or emotion. Think of anger: you feel your muscles tense, your heartbeat accelerate, your temperature rise. The body prepares to fight. This energy, once generated, *must* be released or transformed. If it remains trapped, it begins to burn within, causing suffering.

This is where the term *Vikshipta* becomes relevant. In yogic psychology, *Vikshipta* refers to a scattered or disturbed state of mind—one that is neither stable nor entirely chaotic, but easily distracted and pulled by thoughts, desires, and emotions. It is the condition where a person may *know* they are reacting, may even *wish* to stop, but finds themselves unable to. This is not a weakness—it is a dysfunction of energy regulation between brain and body.

Let's take a real-life example: An office worker named Ankit struggles with overthinking. One day, his manager criticizes him in front of others. For hours afterward, Ankit replays the scene in his mind. His heart races, his stomach tightens, he sweats even though he's sitting still. He *knows* the event is over, but the energy lingers, looping through his body like a storm. He tries to distract himself, but nothing helps. He lies awake at night, his mind restless, his body tense. This is *Vikshipta*—a state where energy released by thoughts overwhelms one's ability to manage or dismiss it.

The key understanding here is this: Thoughts alone don't have the power to cause deep suffering. It is our *identification* with them that releases energy. When a thought arises and we believe in it—whether it's a memory, desire, or fear—it activates the body. That activation becomes feeling. And when we are unable to process or release that energy in a healthy way, it becomes suffering.

This scattered energy—whether it arises as lust, guilt, sorrow, or pride—disturbs the natural balance of the body-mind system. It causes not just emotional disturbance, but physical dysfunction. It can even weaken immunity, affect sleep, and disturb digestion. To live a healthy life, we must become aware of these energies as they arise—not to suppress them, but to recognize and release them consciously.

In conclusion, the connection between thought and body is not just philosophical—it is biological and energetic. Understanding *Vikshipta* is the first step toward returning to balance. Awareness is the medicine. When we can watch our thoughts without getting swept away, when we can feel our emotions without being consumed, we begin to transform energy instead of being trapped by it. This is not just spiritual practice—it is conscious living.

The Fire Within: Understanding Anger, Thought, and Sensory Influence

Anger is one of the most potent emotional energies a human being can experience. It is raw, intense, and deeply reactive. Yet what many fail to recognize is that anger does not begin when we shout at someone or break something—it begins *within*, often long before any external confrontation. In truth, anger burns the person who carries it long before it reaches the person at whom it is directed.

Physiologically, anger activates the body's emergency systems. Hormones like adrenaline surge. The heart beats faster. Muscles tighten. Blood pressure rises. And when this becomes a habitual response—when anger simmers daily, or erupts frequently—it causes actual damage. Over time, nerves can become hypersensitive. Chronic inflammation can develop. In extreme and prolonged cases, conditions like hypertension, neural strain, or even tumor formation may occur. The body is not built to carry anger for long; it is built to release it—consciously and skillfully.

The question arises: where does anger—or any thought, for that matter—originate? The answer lies in our relationship with the outer world. Our body and brain function as receivers, constantly absorbing information through the five senses: sight, sound, smell, taste, and touch. The outer world enters us through these gateways, forming impressions, memories, and triggers. These impressions become the seeds of thought.

This is why ancient wisdom often stated, *"Jaisa ann vaisa mann"*—meaning, *"As is your food, so is your mind."* But the word *"food"* here is not limited to what you eat with your mouth. Everything you consume through your senses—what you see, what you hear, what you experience—becomes food for the mind. If one constantly watches violent media, listens to harsh words, or engages in toxic environments, the mind begins to reflect that energy. Similarly, if one immerses in beauty, music, kindness, or nature, the inner world reflects calm and clarity.

Let us take a relatable example: Imagine a young man, Raj, who is constantly scrolling through social media. Every few minutes, he sees images of luxurious lifestyles, beautiful people, and stimulating content. His brain, stimulated by what he sees, begins to form desires, comparisons, and fantasies. One day, when a real-life situation does not match the fantasy he has been feeding, he feels irritated, restless, and even angry. That anger may not have a clear target—but it's there, simmering beneath the surface. It may explode at someone close to him, or turn inward as frustration or self-doubt.

In this way, our thoughts are not entirely random—they are reactions to the stimuli we absorb from our surroundings. If Raj had spent more time in nature, with honest people, or reading uplifting literature, the quality of his thoughts—and therefore, his emotions—might have been completely different.

Now consider the power of identification. When we identify strongly with a thought—whether it is about food, a person, or an idea—we give it energy. If Raj sees a beautiful girl and instantly feels attraction, his brain produces a thought. But the intensity of his reaction comes not from the image alone—it comes from his *identification* with that thought. He wants, he craves, he feels incomplete without it. That identification turns thought into feeling. And feeling triggers a physical response in the body.

In this cycle—sensation, thought, identification, reaction—our life plays out. And if we are unaware, it leads to imbalance, suffering, and confusion.

To live wisely, then, is to be aware. Aware of what we take in through our senses. Aware of the subtle beginnings of emotion. Aware of the fire of anger before it burns us. Awareness is not a suppression of emotion—it is a soft space where energy is seen, understood, and released without damage.

In conclusion, our bodies are not just biological machines; they are instruments finely tuned to the outer world. Thoughts arise from our sensory experiences, and emotions arise from our identification with those thoughts. To live with balance is to be selective about what we consume—not just with the mouth, but with the eyes, ears, and heart. Because what we allow in, eventually shapes who we are within.

Meditation: The Watchtower of the Self

In the ancient chaos of human life, one truth has quietly echoed through the halls of sages and the hearts of seekers: *The mind is not a battlefield to conquer, but a mirror to observe.*

To control the flood of thoughts our mind constantly generates, we did not build walls or wage wars—we invented **meditation**. Meditation is not a ritual. It is not an act. It is a return. A return to the still center of being, from where all storms pass, but which itself remains untouched.

Why did we invent meditation? Because the outer world is not in our hands. Try to control it, and it will slip through your fingers like sand. Attempt to shape it by force, and you will find yourself shaped by it instead. The more you chase the world, the more it becomes your master.

A king may sit upon a throne, ruling over land and subjects—but if his heart is governed by desire, he is no king. He is a servant, not of his people, but of his own cravings. In truth, **desire rules the world**, not humans. And desire, ironically, is not born from within—it is borrowed, planted by the world outside. What you see, hear, taste, and touch—all these impressions give rise to longing. And every longing is like a leash, pulling you outward, away from your center.

Desire is the fuel of the ego. It is the ego's chariot, riding through illusions, always searching, never arriving. And in its race, it creates noise—mental, emotional, physical noise. We live in that noise, and slowly forget what silence feels like.

Enter meditation.

Meditation is not escape. It is not the rejection of the world—it is the *reorientation* of your gaze. From the outer, to the inner. It is the courageous act of saying: "Let me watch myself first, before I try to fix the world."

At its deepest level, meditation is the **art of doing nothing**—but not in laziness, in awareness. You do not act. You do not react. You sit. You watch. You breathe. You focus—on *nothing*. In that nothingness, a strange thing begins to happen. The mind slows. The thoughts come, but their grip weakens. You start to see them—not as commands to obey, but as clouds passing by. You become the **watcher**.

To watch your thoughts is to dethrone them. To recognize that *you are not your mind, you are the awareness in which the mind moves*. And this is liberation.

Meditation also allows you to feel the energy that moves within you. Is it anger? Is it guilt? Is it sorrow? Let it arise. Do not suppress it. Watch it. Name it, not as judgment, but as awareness. "Ah, here is guilt." "This is the burn of anger." "This tightness—this is fear." In doing this, you don't just name your suffering—you *understand* it. And when understanding is deep, suffering begins to dissolve.

There is a subtle difference between *rest* and *relaxation*. Rest is of the body. Sleep, lying down, idling—all are forms of physical rest. But **relaxation** is deeper. Relaxation is when both the body and the mind are at ease. Meditation is not sleep. It is not unconsciousness. It is total alertness, *without effort.*

In a world that constantly pulls you outward—to buy, to chase, to compare—meditation is a rebellion. A gentle, quiet revolution. You sit down, you close your eyes, and you say: "Let the world be. For now, I am with myself."

This is not a withdrawal. It is the most intimate connection you will ever have—with your own truth, your own silence, your own being.

So the question is not *how* to meditate. The real question is: Are you ready to stop running? To stop chasing desires that were never yours to begin with? Are you ready to meet yourself—not the idea of you, but the you that exists beneath all thoughts?

If yes, then sit. Breathe. Watch. Let the noise fade into the background, and the silence rise like the moon in a dark sky. This is meditation—the watchtower of the Self.

The Pain Trap and the Watcher: A Journey Through Suffering and Self-Mastery

The mind is a wild river. It flows not always in the direction we wish, often crashing against rocks of memory, emotion, and reaction. In this turbulent current, we often drown—not because the water is too deep, but because we forget how to swim. To live consciously, to live mindfully, is to become the **watcher** of this river—not to stop its flow, but to understand it, to respect its power, and to learn how to navigate it.

As a watcher, we must take responsibility—not in the sense of guilt or burden, but with clarity. We must shield ourselves from unnecessary inputs, thoughts, and identifications. For the mind does not create in isolation—it creates in response to what we feed it. Every piece of information, every interaction, every image, sound, or word becomes the raw material for thought. If we are not conscious, we become victims of our own mental creations.

Unconscious identification is the birthplace of suffering. When you deeply identify with a thought, you empower it. Your body begins to react to it. Energy is produced, and depending on how intensely you hold onto the thought, the energy may overwhelm you. If it is not allowed to move, to express, or to release—it can transform into mental disorders, anxiety, depression, or even physical diseases. The mind and body are not separate— they are two instruments of the same symphony.

Take a common yet painful example: you are in a deep relationship, and your partner cheats on you. The betrayal cuts deep. Not just because of what happened—but because of what it shattered: *your belief system*. You had imagined a future, built a story around loyalty, trust, and love. Suddenly, that narrative crumbles, and in its place rises a storm of pain, anger, sorrow, and confusion.

This is not just heartbreak—it is **energetic chaos**. Your body receives the blow of your thoughts. The more you dwell, the more pain is produced. You begin to distrust everyone. The mind becomes a machine of doubt, and every small incident feeds the fire. You drink. You smoke. You fight. You seek distractions, but end up fueling the very pain you wish to escape. Slowly, suffering becomes your habit.

And here lies the most dangerous trap: when **pain becomes familiar**, it becomes *comfortable*. You no longer try to escape it. It lives inside you like a parasite. Now, whatever you do, pain finds a way to grow. This is the pain trap. And it is not external—it is entirely self-fed.

The only escape is *awareness*. Carelessness gives birth to chaos; only mindfulness can birth clarity.

Distracting the mind is a temporary measure. Surrendering to the truth is the real healing. Accept that what is lost is lost. Accept that life moves on. Acceptance is not weakness—it is the strength to stop fighting with yourself. The moment you stop resisting reality, suffering begins to dissolve.

And what is the root of this suffering? Your broken **belief system**. You believed she would be with you forever. You believed loyalty guarantees loyalty in return. These beliefs, when shattered, reveal a brutal truth: the world does not revolve around our expectations. But here's the turning point—when you understand the nature and cause of your suffering, truly understand it, a shift happens. You no longer wish to hurt others. Because you know how pain feels. You become **Dharmik**—not in ritual, but in compassion. You understand that hurting another is hurting yourself.

This is the beginning of **character**. Not built by image or status, but by inner realization. Your habits become your character. Your choices become your destiny. Even suffering, when digested with awareness, becomes a teacher. After trauma, you learn. You learn not to invest emotions blindly. You learn to create boundaries. You learn not to cling. Even the betrayal of a lover can become the doorway to wisdom, if you are watching carefully.

But let us not be naïve. The mind is, by its very nature, uncontrollable. Trying to fully control it is like trying to control the wind. Yet you can become the *anchor*. You may not stop every thought, but you can stop identifying with every thought. That is the difference between madness and mastery.

In the end, **suffering is not your enemy**. It is a mirror. A test. A fire that can burn you—or forge you. The choice is yours. Will you run from it, or sit with it and listen?

Meditation. Awareness. Acceptance. These are not spiritual accessories. They are survival tools in the storm of the modern mind.

And if, even after all the chaos, you can look at someone who wronged you and say, "I will not cause the same pain to another,"—then you have not only healed. You have evolved.

The Fire and the Bridge: An Essay on Meditation and Mindfulness

Meditation does not begin when you sit quietly and close your eyes. Rather, it begins **when the light of awareness touches your being**. Until then, all effort is a journey through fire. The path of the yogi is *Agnipath*—a path forged in the inner fire of discipline and transformation. It scorches away the impurities, confronts the illusions, and tests the will. But when the fire has cleansed you, a subtle transformation takes place. The path which once burned becomes *Ram-sethu*—a bridge, not of stones, but of realization. This bridge carries the seeker from the limited to the limitless, from the individual to the *Virat*—the cosmic form, the universal Self.

What is Meditation?

Meditation is not an escape from the world, nor a technique meant to silence the mind forcibly. It is a profound **sādhanā**—a dedicated practice aimed at inner perfection. Among all spiritual disciplines, this is the seed from which all other attainments emerge. Whether one follows devotion (*bhakti*), knowledge (*jñāna*), or action (*karma*), meditation remains the silent core, the center where all paths converge.

To meditate is to **begin understanding yourself deeply**, with honesty and clarity. Not through books, not through someone else's words, but through a conscious observation of your own mind and being.

Mindfulness: The Gateway to Meditation

When you begin applying this awareness to your daily life, it takes the form of mindfulness. Often misunderstood as mere focus or attention, **mindfulness is actually alert consciousness**. It is the art of seeing clearly, without filters or preconceptions.

The surface level of mindfulness may appear simple: being present, evaluating right from wrong, observing your behavior. But this is only the first gate.

Imagine a man about to commit theft. In that moment, he becomes alert, aware that someone might be watching. His senses sharpen, his mind becomes focused. This temporary state of heightened awareness is what you need to develop consciously—not out of fear, but out of responsibility. Just as the thief becomes conscious of the outer consequences, the meditator becomes conscious of **inner consequences**—what effect each thought, word, or action has on the soul.

But the mind resists this. Its tendency is toward **forgetfulness**, toward inertia. It whispers, "Everything is fine as it is. Why bother?" This is the inner narcotic. Slowly, one slips into a mechanical mode of living. One forgets why something is being done, what choices led here, and where it is heading.

Forgetfulness and the Seduction of Light

Forgetfulness is seductive because it is effortless. It requires no effort to drift, to surrender to the mind's autopilot. In this unconscious state, the individual becomes like an app handed over to God—as if saying, "Let life drive itself. I'll just sit back." But in this surrender, there is no awareness, only abandonment.

Sometimes, even too much light can become blinding. When your mind is bombarded by information, emotion, and constant stimulation, it creates a kind of spiritual blindness. Just as the eyes cannot see in excessive light, the inner eye cannot see when overwhelmed by the noise of thoughts.

Eventually, one closes their eyes to this chaos—and even then, they cannot see. In darkness or light, there is blindness unless there is **conscious seeing**.

The Observer and the Thought

Meditation begins when you start watching your thoughts—not analyzing or judging them, just watching. This act of watching is the **awakening of the witness**, the *sakshi*. You begin to realize: "These thoughts are not me. I am the one who sees them."

This shift is subtle but powerful. Once you identify as the observer, the thoughts lose their grip. You are no longer pulled into their currents unconsciously.

When a thought arises—anger, for instance—it brings with it a certain energy. If you identify with the anger, that energy floods your system. Your heartbeat rises, your breath shortens, your body prepares to fight. The thought then *possesses* you.

But if you remain the observer, you may notice the same thought arise, but it passes like a cloud. Its power does not enter you because you are not feeding it.

A Live Example: The Tension at Work

Imagine you are at your workplace. A colleague speaks to you in a rude tone. Immediately, a rush of anger surges through you. A thought arises: *"He always disrespects me. I should give it back to him."*

In a state of forgetfulness, this thought controls your reaction. You respond with anger, escalate the conflict, and later regret your words.

But now imagine you are practicing mindfulness. The same situation happens, but instead of reacting, you observe the thought: *"He disrespects me."* You do not suppress it, nor do you act on it. You just watch.

In that moment of watching, **a space opens**. In that space, clarity arises. You may see that his behavior is not about you—it is about his own stress. Or you may still choose to respond firmly, but without aggression. The difference is that now *you are in command*, not the thought.

This is meditation—not something you do apart from life, but something that begins to transform life itself.

The Last Glimpse

The culmination of meditation is what the mystics call **the last glimpse**—the moment where the seer realizes that they are not what they see. Not the thoughts, not the emotions, not even the body. The one who observes, silently and eternally, is the true self.

When this seeing becomes constant, not only in meditation but in the midst of daily life, then you walk through Agnipath, but it no longer burns. It becomes *Ram-sethu*, a divine bridge taking you from the shore of illusion to the shore of the infinite.

In this state, you are no longer lost in light or darkness. You *see*—and that seeing is freedom.

Beyond Thought: Understanding Mindfulness, Memory, and Experience

We live most of our lives guided by thoughts— some conscious, many unconscious. At times, we deliberately choose a thought and allow our attention to settle on it. This conscious choice is what we call **mindfulness**. It is not merely being aware of what we are doing; it is the act of intentionally choosing where our mind will rest, and as a result, how our body will respond.

For instance, if you choose a peaceful thought, your body responds with calm. If you focus on a stressful thought, your muscles tighten, your breath shortens. The body follows the mind, and the mind follows thought. This subtle process plays out every day in our lives.

But there is something even deeper—**the one who chooses** the thought. This awareness, this inner observer that selects, rejects, and watches thoughts unfold, is beyond thought and even beyond mindfulness. Because if you can observe a thought, and apply or remove your mind from it, then surely **you are not the mind**. You are that which sees the mind in motion.

The Loop of Thought and Memory

Let us look closer at how a thought becomes part of our life. Suppose you go to college every day. Initially, this thought is new and needs to be remembered consciously: *"I have to go to college at 9 AM."* Over time, this repetition stores the thought in your memory. Eventually, even without actively thinking about it, your body and mind prepare automatically. You wake up, get dressed, and leave—like a program running on schedule.

This is not random—it is the **power of memory**. When a thought repeats enough, it becomes part of your habitual pattern. Memory, in this sense, is not just the past—it is an active force that returns to us at specific times to shape our behavior. You don't have to "think" about college every morning—it just happens.

This leads to a deeper understanding: **habits, thoughts, and knowledge do not possess their own sense of morality**. They are tools—neither good nor bad in themselves. They do not inherently know what is right or wrong.

o How Do We Know What Is Right or Wrong?

This brings us to **experience**. While the mind stores memories, it is experience that interprets them. Experience is the outcome of having lived through consequences, either personally or through the wisdom of others. It's not just knowledge—it is **embodied wisdom**.

Take a simple example. You are walking under the hot sun, and your throat is dry. The only thing in your mind is water. You see a stream by the roadside. You pause. *Should I drink from it?*

Even though your body craves water, a deeper voice within holds you back. You remember—or perhaps were taught—that water from a stream may be unsafe. This moment, where desire is checked by insight, is the fruit of experience.

Experience transforms memory into wisdom.

Fire as a Teacher

Consider fire. If a child touches it once, they feel pain. That is the first layer of experience: *Fire burns*. This experience becomes a long-lasting memory that automatically activates whenever fire is seen. But over time, more layers are added.

You don't just remember that fire burns. You understand that fire can cook food, provide warmth, light up darkness, forge tools. You also learn that keeping a certain distance from fire lets you benefit from it safely.

This deeper understanding—knowing how close is too close—is not taught by thought alone. It is cultivated through **direct and indirect experience**. Thus, fire becomes not just a danger, but a **multidimensional teacher**. It is through this lens that we understand the world—not by avoiding experience, but by learning through it.

The Inner Mechanism of Wisdom

When you see fire, and a thousand associations arise—burns, warmth, cooking, danger, comfort—that is experience stored as **deep memory**. Unlike fleeting thoughts, experience stays. It guides you even when you're not consciously thinking.

And this mechanism works with every aspect of life—relationships, food, time, silence, even spirituality.

What truly matters is how you interpret your memory through the lens of awareness. Without awareness, memory can trap you in old patterns. With awareness, it becomes your guide.

The Silent Witness

In all of this, a deeper self remains untouched. It is the one who chooses thoughts, who reflects on memories, and who learns from experience. This self is not your mind—it is your **conscious presence**.

Mindfulness is the bridge. Memory is the storage. Experience is the interpreter. But **the self beyond** all of these is the seer—the one who watches it all and remains free.

When you begin living from that center, your life transforms. You are no longer pushed around by unconscious habits or fleeting thoughts. You begin to act from clarity, and your experience becomes the soil in which wisdom flowers.

Mindfulness and the Mirage of Thought: A Philosophical Journey Into Presence

In the vast theatre of the mind, thoughts rise like actors on a stage—each playing their role, each demanding the spotlight. But few pause to ask: **Who is the one watching this play? Who is the silent observer behind the curtain?**

To understand mindfulness, one must first recognize an astonishing truth—**all your thoughts are ghosts**. They are not born of the now. They either haunt you from the past or seduce you with visions of the future. A memory dressed in nostalgia, a dream draped in hope, a regret curled in silence—these are the forms they take. They knock on the doors of your mind and beg to be let in. And once they enter, they want to merge with you. To become *you*.

But there is a way to stay awake amidst this parade of illusions. It begins with awareness.

The First Phase: The Art of Choosing Thoughts

The first stage of mindfulness is simple, yet revolutionary—it is the act of **choosing your thoughts consciously**.

The modern mind is like a crowded marketplace where every thought is a seller calling out, waving, trying to attract attention. Mindfulness teaches you to walk through this market with awareness—not buying every product, not getting lost in the crowd. You become a discerning witness.

This stage is rooted in experience. For instance, when a negative thought arises—perhaps anger, fear, or doubt—you pause and reflect: *"Have I gone down this road before? What was the result?"* Based on that reflection, you either engage with the thought or let it pass.

This choosing is the first empowerment of mindfulness. It is not about suppressing thought, but **standing apart** from it. Watching it. Evaluating it. Responding—not reacting.

As you practice this, a certain clarity begins to dawn. You begin to notice how deeply your life has been driven by habitual thought-patterns—by ghosts of what was or fantasies of what might be.

This is the gateway.

The Second Phase: Freedom From Thought

Once you learn to watch and choose your thoughts, a deeper possibility opens: **what if you stopped choosing altogether? What if you simply stopped feeding the mind?**

This is the second phase of mindfulness. Here, the goal is not to manage thought—but to **move beyond it**. It is to release the mind from its compulsive storytelling. It is to come home to the *now*.

"Live in the present," the sages have said. But this is not a slogan—it is a practice. A return. A shedding of all mental clothing. For in the present, **thought has no role**. It cannot exist. The mind cannot create anything *here*. The moment you fully enter the present, thought disappears like mist before the rising sun.

But this second phase is not easy. It cannot be done in the chaos of action. You must first come into stillness. Into **relaxation**—not merely of body, but of being.

Sit. Breathe. Withdraw gently. The eyes may close—not to shut out the world, but to see the world within. And here begins the real challenge.

The Challenge of Emptiness

As thought begins to fade, something unexpected arises—**a strange emptiness**.

At first, it may feel like a void. A kind of dizziness. A silence too loud to bear. The mind becomes uneasy.

The ego, which fed on thought, begins to panic. For without thoughts, **the ego begins to die**.

Thoughts are the lifeblood of the ego. Every opinion, every fear, every story it tells about "me" and "mine"—these are the bricks of its house. Take them away, and it stands naked, trembling.

It begins to resist. It throws distractions. It whispers doubts. It may even create new spiritual thoughts to preserve its relevance. *"Look how peaceful I am!"* it says. But even this is a thought. A trap.

The ego cannot survive in the present. Because the present has **no story**. It just is.

In this silence, you meet your aloneness. Not loneliness—but the pure, sacred state of being **with no reference point**. No identity. No role. No narrative. Just *being*.

Philosophical Reflections: Who Am I Without Thought?

This brings us to a timeless philosophical question: **What remains when thought ends?**

Descartes said, *"I think, therefore I am."* But the mystics would laugh gently at this. They would say,

"No, dear friend. You are—not because you think, but because you can witness thought."

The Upanishads called this witness the *Sakshi*—the silent observer behind the drama of the mind. Buddha called it *Sunyata*—emptiness, full of awareness. In Zen, it is known as *no-mind*. In all traditions, the insight is the same: **You are not your thoughts. You are the space in which thoughts arise and dissolve.**

When you touch this space, you enter a new dimension of living. You do not become inactive or dull. On the contrary, you become *radiantly alive*. Because now, your actions are not born of compulsion—they are born of clarity. You speak not to impress, but to express. You act not to prove, but to serve. You love not to possess, but to rejoice.

A Living Example: The Thought of Death

Let's take a practical example. Imagine you are sitting quietly and suddenly the thought arises: *"One day, I will die."* Normally, this might lead to fear, distraction, or morbid curiosity.

But if you are mindful, you observe: *"Ah, here comes the thought of death. It wants my attention."*

You don't run from it. You don't indulge it. You simply **watch**.

And as you watch, the thought fades. In its place comes a quiet, spacious awareness. You're not dead. You're *here*. Breathing. Present. And in that presence, death loses its sting. It becomes just another thought—not a tyrant, but a passing cloud.

This is freedom. This is mindfulness deepened into presence.

Conclusion: From Thought to Truth

Mindfulness begins as an act of watching thoughts. It matures into the courage to let go of them. In this letting go, a deeper presence emerges—silent, formless, alive.

The ego resists. The mind rebels. But if you persist, a great truth is revealed:

You are not the thinker.
You are not even the thoughts.
You are the sky in which the clouds of thought appear and vanish.

And once you know this—not as theory, but as lived experience—you are free.

The Shock of Seeing: Meditation and the Illusion of Ahankaar Bhram

Just as a fisherman casts ashes into a pond to obscure the waters while something remains hidden beneath, so too does *Ahankaar Bhram*—the illusion of ego—veil the truth of our lives. It shows us a version of living, a face that appears genuine but is born of deception. It tells us what life *should* look like, how *you* should look—successful, desirable, strong, unbreakable. It constructs a mask so subtly that we begin to believe it is our true face. Meditation, however, unravels this mask. It does not simply reveal another face—it reveals that there is no face at all, just pure seeing.

To meditate is to begin the difficult process of emptying. Not just the mind, but the self. In true meditation, one sits not as a person with a goal but as consciousness watching itself. You don't *do* meditation, you become meditation.

And when you start to observe this illusion—the ego, the compulsive thinker—there is a strange shock. A shock much like how a garden might respond if it could suddenly become aware of its own growing—seeing the way each leaf uncurls, how the sun bends its path, how water changes its very shape. Meditation brings that same startling awareness. You begin to *see* every movement of your thought, every twitch of desire, every subtle escape of the mind.

This shock is not gentle. It is not poetic at first. It is like hunger that forces you to learn how to eat. The same desperation a starving man feels when he learns to beg, borrow, or steal just to survive, you will feel in your search to escape the prison of your mind. It may bring you shame, because your illusions will fight to stay alive. But if you endure it, a strange joy will begin to rise—a joy not born of pleasure but of clarity. And with it, a new kind of power: *control over your inner world*.

The real crisis is not the presence of thought, but the loss of self within thought. We often don't realize how far we've drifted until it's too late. One thought leads to another, like stepping stones into a whirlpool. At some point, we find ourselves drowning and cannot stop—even if we desperately want to. There is no "off" switch for the mind. Even when the body begs for sleep, the mind keeps playing like a broken radio stuck between stations.

Meditation is that rare manual no one gave us, the one that teaches us how to silence the noise, how to step out of the whirlpool.

In the second stage of meditation, this deepening silence is often referred to as the *no signal state*. Just like a television that is powered on but receives no transmission, the mind becomes quiet, still, and yet alert. The channels of thought are shut down. There is only static—and even that begins to fade. But remember, in this state, the mind is still *on*. The ego may try to return at any moment. The signal can break through again at any time, trying to reinsert its drama.

This is a delicate and vital stage. Here, you may feel emptiness—not the peaceful kind at first, but a hollowness that unsettles you. The ego interprets this as a kind of death. It panics, fights, and tries to seduce you with comforting thoughts. But it is precisely by walking through this inner desert, without chasing an oasis, that you begin to taste real freedom.

Stage Three: The Ocean of the Self – Atma-Gyan and the Death of Ego

If the second stage of meditation is the silent mind—a television with no signal, humming with emptiness—then the third stage is the disappearance of the television itself. This is the state of **Atma-Gyan**: the direct experience of the self, not as a separate entity, but as pure awareness beyond body, thought, or identity.

At this stage, the boundaries begin to dissolve. You no longer disengage merely from thoughts; you begin to detach from the very body that housed those thoughts. The sense of being "someone" inside the body starts to fade. This is not a metaphor—it is a real phenomenological shift. The body becomes irrelevant. Time becomes irrelevant. Space softens. What remains is awareness, a kind of formless perception that does not need an observer. It is the flame watching itself burn.

But this is not a peaceful transition. It is disorder before reordering. It is chaos before stillness.

To leave behind thoughts is to silence the noise of the world. But to leave behind the body is to silence the self's last illusion of security. This is the threshold of fear—the point where the ego meets its inevitable end. And make no mistake: the ego does not die quietly. It clings. It bargains. It schemes. It seduces.

This is why the third stage takes time. Not in clock-time, but in the unfolding of inner seasons. For most, it is terrifying to forget the story of "me." Memories will try to return. Identity will knock on the door. The fear of death will whisper in your ear. "You're going too far," it says. "Come back. You're disappearing." And yes, you are.

Because in this sacred vanishing, the ego dies. And when it dies, the world as you *knew* it also dies. All the meanings, attachments, ambitions, comparisons, judgments—these collapse. And what is left is not silence. It is not even peace. What remains is **total freedom**.

This is the final defeat of fear—not because fear is fought, but because the one who fears is no longer there.

In this space, the mind becomes vast. It is no longer a pond reflecting passing clouds of thought; it becomes the ocean. Now imagine throwing a stone into that ocean. Does it disturb it? Do ripples reach the shore? The world throws its stones, but nothing stirs. This is the nature of the liberated mind. Thoughts may arise, but they find no place to rest. They dissolve as quickly as they come.

Here, **loneliness becomes your teacher**. Not the loneliness born of abandonment, but the existential aloneness of the mystic—the one who has stepped beyond the social dream. Loneliness transforms. What was once a thorn of suffering becomes a thorn of awakening. In that sharpness, you begin to understand that loneliness is not a lack—it is a spacious presence untouched by crowd or company. The yogi walks through this desert willingly. And in doing so, the thirst for desire is slowly quenched.

Desire doesn't die by suppression; it dies by sublimation. Its energy is no longer chaotic—it becomes distilled, like vapor turning into rain. The once restless anxiety of "what next?" becomes a quiet joy in "what is." You no longer chase bliss; you become its resting place.

But beware—this is the point where the ego makes its most cunning attempt. Stripped of its identity, it may take the form of a "spiritual self." It may whisper thoughts of superiority, thoughts of "now I am enlightened," or "I have arrived." This is its last trap: spiritual pride. If you catch it, you are free. If not, it builds a golden cage that looks like liberation but is only another form of bondage.

The examination continues. The scrutiny deepens. Until finally, the thoughts that once governed your life become nothing but echoes in a vast cave. Sick thoughts—those born of fear, guilt, shame, lust for control—begin to vanish. Not suppressed, but simply *irrelevant*. The soul now breathes fully.

Here, for the first time, **you begin to understand death**. Not as an ending, but as a doorway. You see that death is not opposite to life, but to ego. The body may still be alive, but the "you" who once feared death is no more. It is this realization that all mystics, saints, and sages have pointed to.

In this state, the world dissolves into what the Buddha called *Nirvana*—the extinguishing of the flame of self. Mahavira named it *Kevalya*—absolute knowledge untouched by perception. Both speak of the same truth, the same void, the same light. Their languages differ, but their silence is one.

And in that silence, you become the ocean. The waves of thought may rise and fall, but you no longer rise and fall with them.

Stage Four: Ardh-Samadhi – Union with Nature, the Divine Silence

After the ego has dissolved, after all thoughts, desires, and attachments have vanished into the void of the third stage, what remains? **Not the mind. Not the self. Not even the witness.** What remains is **presence**—a silence so deep that it cannot be spoken, only lived. This is the fourth stage of meditation: **Ardh-Samadhi**.

In this state, even the body no longer needs to function in its usual way. One sits not because one chooses to, but because there is no chooser left. The body remains still for hours, even days. Time no longer registers because there is no internal measurement, no mental clock ticking, no "I" waiting for something to happen. It is like a **TV that is not just on "no signal" but now completely switched off**, unplugged from both the world and the self.

This is the "switch-off state," not of unconsciousness but of **super-consciousness**—the paradox where you are fully awake without being anyone.

Here, the mind is not a pond or even an ocean—it is **the sky itself**, unbounded, still, and everywhere. All thoughts that once served even the body's survival now dissolve. Breathing becomes slow. The heart beats with nature. There is no resistance, no separation. This is not death, but the total cessation of the illusion of separateness. You do not feel one with nature—you *are* nature. Your breath is the wind, your heartbeat is the pulse of the cosmos. There is no longer a meditator—only **meditation** remains.

This Is the Birth of the Divine Within

Here, **love, kindness, and truth** become your very essence. You don't practice compassion—it flows from you like fragrance from a flower. Now, whatever you say is **truth**, not because of knowledge, but because it rises from the soul—the place where all truth resides.

This is the **state of God-realization**, of divine absorption.

When one reaches here, the very **purpose of returning to the world dissolves**. You do not want to get up—not because of desire, but because the "you" who would get up no longer has any function. If someone physically lifts you, you may return for a while. But the pull of that inner ocean is so deep, so comforting, that worldly reality appears like a distant, faint dream.

Here, the words of **Buddha** ring clear: *"Life is suffering."* But what he meant was not that life is misery—it is that as long as you are entangled in desire, ego, and illusion, suffering persists. But when you transcend, the suffering ends, not by fixing life, but by going beyond it.

One Truth, Many Faces

All the great masters reached this point—**not in theory, but in lived experience**. Their words differ, but their **truth is one**.

- **Buddha** called it **Nirvana**, the extinguishing of the flame of ego.

- **Mahavira** called it **Kevalya**, the state of infinite perception.

- **Jesus** said, *"I am the Son of God,"* not as an identity, but as a realization that he and the divine were not separate. He saw love in all beings—his message became **compassion**.

- **Krishna**, seeing the divine everywhere and within, declared, *"I am God."* His was a state of cosmic play—*leela*.

- **Muhammad** said, *"I am the Messenger of God,"* because he saw that the truth he received was not personal—it was a transmission of the One.

Each was looking into the same mirror of truth—only the **reflections were described in different languages**.

As the mystic **Rumi** wrote,
"The lamps are different, but the Light is the same."

A Living Example: Ramana Maharshi

Let us take a real-life example: **Ramana Maharshi**, a young boy from Tamil Nadu, India. One day, at the age of sixteen, he was seized by a sudden and overwhelming fear of death. But instead of running, he lay down and consciously observed his fear. He asked, *"Who is dying?"* and slowly realized, *"The body dies, but I am not the body."*

This self-inquiry plunged him into a deep **samadhi-like state** that lasted for hours. From that day forward, he had no interest in the world. He moved to the holy mountain of **Arunachala**, where he sat in silence, completely absorbed in the Self. People were drawn to him because in his presence they felt peace, truth, and divinity. He spoke rarely, but every word he spoke came from that **divine silence**.

Ramana's life became the embodiment of the fourth stage. He had no identity, no ambition, no fear. Just presence—like an unplugged TV glowing with the last light of eternity.

The Ineffable Unity

So what remains after everything is gone? **Nothing. And everything.**

Words collapse here. Descriptions fail. You are not empty—you are **emptiness**. You are not loving— you are **love**. You do not know the truth—you are **truth itself**. And the self, which once wandered the world looking for meaning, has **become the meaning**.

This is liberation. This is *moksha*. This is *fanaa*, *nirvana*, *kevalya*, *Christ-consciousness*—whatever name we give it, the essence is the same.

And once this is tasted, —**who wants to return?**